IMAGINATION'S OTHER PLACE

Compiled by Helen Plotz

IMAGINATION'S OTHER PLACE
UNTUNE THE SKY
POEMS OF EMILY DICKINSON
THE EARTH IS THE LORD'S

IMAGINATION'S OTHER PLACE

Poems of Science and
Mathematics

COMPILED BY Helen Plotz

ILLUSTRATED WITH WOOD ENGRAVINGS BY
Clare Leighton

THOMAS Y. CROWELL COMPANY
NEW YORK

Imagination's Other Place: Poems About Science and Mathematics
Copyright 1955 by Harper & Row, Publishers, Inc.
Printed in the U.S.A. All rights reserved.
Library of Congress Catalog Card Number: 55-9216
ISBN 0-690-43413-8
ISBN 0-690-04700-2 (lib. bdg.)

---

*Grateful acknowledgment is made to the following publishers and authors
for permission to reprint copyrighted material:*

ABBOTT LABORATORIES AND MARIANNE MOORE for "The Staff of Aesculapius" by Marianne Moore.

THE ATLANTIC MONTHLY AND LEONORA SPEYER for "X-Ray" by Leonora Speyer.

A. & C. BLACK, LTD., for the Canadian permission for twelve stanzas from "No Single Thing Abides" by Titus Lucretius Carus and translated by W. H. Mallock.

BRANDT & BRANDT for excerpt from "Journal" in *Mine the Harvest* by Edna St. Vincent Millay, published by Harper & Brothers, copyright 1954 by Norma Millay Ellis; for "Euclid Alone Has Looked on Beauty Bare" from *The Harp-Weaver and Other Poems* by Edna St. Vincent Millay, published by Harper & Brothers, copyright 1920, 1948 by Edna St. Vincent Millay; and for "Metropolitan Nightmare" by Stephen Vincent Benét, originally published in *The New Yorker* magazine, copyright 1933 by Stephen Vincent Benét.

CHICAGO TRIBUNE for "The Dinosaur" by Bert Leston Taylor.

ELIZABETH COATSWORTH for her poem "The Pleiades," published by Harper & Brothers.

MR. ARTHUR DOBELL for "Thanksgiving for the Body" by Thomas Traherne, from *The Poetical Works of Thomas Traherne*, published by P. J. and A. E. Dobell.

DODD, MEAD & COMPANY for the American permission for twelve stanzas from "No Single Thing Abides" by Titus Lucretius Carus, translated by W. H. Mallock.

E. P. DUTTON & CO., INC., for selections from *Collected Poems* by Louise Townsend Nicholl published by E. P. Dutton & Company, Inc.: "A Different Speech," copyright 1950 as "Dispatch" by *The Saturday Review of Literature*; "Ark of the Covenant," copyright 1949 by *The Saturday Review of Literature*; "The Shape of the Heart," copyright October–November 1942, by *The Poetry Chap-Book*. For "Physical Geography" by Louise Townsend Nicholl, from *Water & Light*, copyright 1939 by E. P. Dutton & Co., Inc. For "Homage to the Philosopher" by Babette Deutsch, copyright 1953 by Babette Deutsch; from *Animal, Vegetable, Mineral* published by E. P. Dutton & Co., Inc. For "Heart Specialist" by Elias Lieberman, copyright 1951 by *Spirit, A Magazine of Poetry*; from *To My Brothers Everywhere* published by E. P. Dutton & Co., Inc. For "Ode to the Hayden Planetarium" by Arthur Guiterman, from *Lyric Laughter*, copyright 1939 by E. P. Dutton & Co., Inc.

FABER AND FABER, LTD., and WALTER DE LA MARE for the Canadian permission for "The Dunce" by Walter de la Mare. Faber and Faber, Ltd., for the Canadian permission for the selection from "Little Gidding" from *Four Quartets* by T. S. Eliot; for excerpts from "Numbers and Faces" from *Nones* by W. H. Auden; and for "The Motion of the Earth" from *The Pot Geranium* by Norman Nicholson.

TO Milton
AND TO Our Children

Elizabeth, Paul, Sarah,
and John

PREFACE

"Man may die of imagination," said Chaucer; he might well have said that men live by imagination as well, for man alone possesses the gift of imagination, the gift of wonder. Only man, of all living creatures, lives and dies for ideas and symbols, and not by instinct or chance alone. In the rest of the animal kingdom many of our faculties and even our achievements appear in some form. Division of labor, communication, care of the young, war-making, and architecture all exist among the birds and beasts and even the insects. Many animals have lived in caves but only man has drawn pictures on the walls.

We do not know now whether the man who drew the pictures on the wall was the first scientist or the first artist. It may be that he was both, for science and art—or poetry, if you will—are alike dedicated to exploring and questioning. There can be little doubt that the drawings arose from man's wonder at the things about him, perhaps partly from fear and partly from the desire to communicate a unique experience.

This desire to communicate is basic both to science and to poetry. Both scientist and poet may perceive certain truths intuitively; the scientist sets about to verify these truths by experiment; the poet attempts to express them through the words and rhythms of common speech. For both, order is the ultimate goal. The scientist seeks to find the order of the universe through the discipline of experiment; the poet, through the discipline of language. He seeks to capture and transmit his vision of order or his despair at disorder.

Poets and scientists have another link between them. Poets have always been interested in scientific discoveries and the men who made them. Sometimes, indeed, poets have anticipated the scientists and have written about such topics as evolution and space-time with miraculous insight and foresight.

The poems collected here have to do with science and mathematics and with the men who shaped these fields. Not all of these poems are reverent or even serious, for poets need not always look at the world right side up. The divisions are: first, astronomy and geography; second, physics, mathematics, and chemistry; third, biology and medicine. Last of all is the section devoted to great men of science, men whose vision, no less than that of the poets, has illuminated the universe for us.

A modern poet, May Sarton, says, in tribute to her father, George Sarton, a great historian of science:

> "And sacred order has been always won
> From chaos by some burning faithful one
> Whose human bones have ached as if with fever
> To bring you to these high triumphant places."

One of the greatest of scientists, who had himself reached the high triumphant places, spoke of his work with a humility and sincerity that reaches us even now, over the many years that have gone by since he made his discoveries. I think that we may best begin this book with these words of Sir Isaac Newton: "I do not know what I may appear to the world; but to myself I seem to have been only like a boy playing on the seashore and diverting myself in now and then finding a smoother pebble or a prettier shell than ordinary whilst the great ocean of truth lay all undiscovered before me."

ACKNOWLEDGMENTS

I can list only a few of the many friends who have helped me; my thanks go to all who listened to me and who wished me well.

My first and deepest thanks to my husband and our two older children who made me read about science in self-defense so that I could learn enough to follow their lively discussions. Their enthusiasm has been boundless.

Some of the ideas behind this anthology have been germinating since my college days and I should especially like to thank Professor Jane Swenarton who tried to teach me the principles of criticism, and Professor Helen Lockwood in whose English J class I first learned of the ties between science and poetry. Professor Barbara Swain of Vassar, whom I did not know then, has kindly made available to me invaluable source material.

Fannie Gittleman hitched Pegasus to a wagon for me and has relieved me of all burdensome detail.

Since I first came to the Children's Book Committee of The Child Study Association of America, Josette Frank, Staff Adviser to the committee, has fortified me and encouraged me.

My thanks to Ruth Berkowsky of the mathematics department of Erasmus Hall High School for giving me access to the files of *Papyrus,* the magazine of her XYZ Club. Professor Alice Langellier of Finch College suggested the two sonnets by Sully-Prudhomme and Dr. William Dock translated them with grace. Bernard Jaffe, teacher and chronicler of science, read the introductions with scientific regard for accuracy. Mary Wing let me browse in her fine library of English and American poetry, and Dorothy Plum gave me the freedom of the Vassar College library.

To Theresa Wolfson Wood for many constructive suggestions and for sympathetic and careful reading of the entire manuscript I am deeply indebted.

CONTENTS

SECTION 1 · In the Beginning

AUGURIES OF INNOCENCE   5
  William Blake

from FOUR QUARTETS   6
  T. S. Eliot

A VISION   7
  Henry Vaughan

"ATOM FROM ATOM"   8
  Ralph Waldo Emerson

from "NO SINGLE THING ABIDES"   9
  Titus Lucretius Carus

from PROMETHEUS UNBOUND   12
  Percy Bysshe Shelley

from GENESIS   14

"GOD'S FIRST CREATURE WAS LIGHT"   17
  Winifred Welles

THE TORTOISE IN ETERNITY   18
  Elinor Wylie

THE GOD OF GALAXIES   19
  Mark Van Doren

ONCE A CHILD   21
  Emily Dickinson

from TROILUS AND CRESSIDA   22
    William Shakespeare

from HUDIBRAS   23
    Samuel Butler

MY FATHER'S WATCH   24
    John Ciardi

THIS DIM AND PTOLEMAIC MAN   25
    John Peale Bishop

A DIFFERENT SPEECH   26
    Louise Townsend Nicholl

GO FLY A SAUCER   27
    David McCord

ODE TO THE HAYDEN PLANETARIUM   29
    Arthur Guiterman

FOR THE CONJUNCTION OF TWO PLANETS   30
    Adrienne Cecile Rich

THE PLEIADES   31
    Elizabeth Coatsworth

URSA MAJOR   32
    James Kirkup

from THE PRINCESS   33
    Alfred, Lord Tennyson

WEALTH   34
    Ralph Waldo Emerson

ARK OF THE COVENANT   36
    Louise Townsend Nicholl

REVOLUTION   37
    A. E. Housman

THE MOTION OF THE EARTH 38
  Norman Nicholson

from JOB 39

from ROCK 42
  Kathleen Raine

SHELLS 43
  Kathleen Raine

from WATER 44
  Kathleen Raine

from JOB 45

from THE CLOUD 46
  Percy Bysshe Shelley

"LOW-ANCHORED CLOUD" 49
  Henry Thoreau

TO A SNOW-FLAKE 50
  Francis Thompson

WEATHER WORDS 51
  David McCord

PHYSICAL GEOGRAPHY 52
  Louise Townsend Nicholl

CONTINENT'S END 53
  Robinson Jeffers

EPISTLE TO BE LEFT IN THE EARTH 55
  Archibald MacLeish

SECTION 2 · The Kingdom of Number

"SCIENCE IN GOD" 61
  Robert Herrick

from REPLY TO MR. WORDSWORTH   62
    Archibald MacLeish

THE WHEEL   63
    Sully-Prudhomme

RELATIVITY   64
    Anonymous

APOSTROPHIC NOTES FROM THE NEW-WORLD PHYSICS   65
    E. B. White

FOUR QUARTZ CRYSTAL CLOCKS   67
    Marianne Moore

THE NAKED WORLD   69
    Sully-Prudhomme

THE LABORATORY MIDNIGHT   70
    Reuel Denney

from RELIQUES   71
    Edmund Blunden

MATHEMATICS OR THE GIFT OF TONGUES   72
    Anna Hempstead Branch

"EUCLID ALONE HAS LOOKED ON BEAUTY BARE"   75
    Edna St. Vincent Millay

TULIPS   76
    Padraic Colum

"TO THINK THAT TWO AND TWO ARE FOUR"   77
    A. E. Housman

ARITHMETIC   78
    Carl Sandburg

"THERE WAS AN OLD MAN WHO SAID, 'DO'"   79
    Anonymous

"THERE WAS A YOUNG MAN FROM TRINITY"   80
    Anonymous

EUCLID   81
    Vachel Lindsay

E = MC²   82
    Morris Bishop

THE STARFISH   83
    Robert P. Tristram Coffin

THE ICOSASPHERE   84
    Marianne Moore

from THE PRELUDE   85
    William Wordsworth

from HUDIBRAS   86
    Samuel Butler

PLANE GEOMETRY   87
    Emma Rounds

"THE POINT, THE LINE, THE SURFACE AND SPHERE"   89
    Claude Bragdon

ENTROPY   90
    Theodore Spencer

from NUMBERS AND FACES   91
    W. H. Auden

SECTION 3 · Both Man and Bird and Beast

"THE FORCE THAT THROUGH THE GREEN FUSE
DRIVES THE FLOWER"   98
    Dylan Thomas

MESSAGE FROM HOME   99
    Kathleen Raine

IF THEY SPOKE   102
Mark Van Doren

COLD-BLOODED CREATURES   103
Elinor Wylie

INNATE HELIUM   104
Robert Frost

THE MASKED SHREW   105
Isabella Gardner

"I SAW A PEACOCK"   106
Anonymous

"OUR LITTLE KINSMEN"   107
Emily Dickinson

THE SPIDER   108
Robert P. Tristram Coffin

from THE TRIUMPH OF THE WHALE   110
Charles Lamb

VARIATION ON A SENTENCE   111
Louise Bogan

THE DINOSAUR   112
Bert Leston Taylor

AT WOODWARD'S GARDENS   113
Robert Frost

METROPOLITAN NIGHTMARE   115
Stephen Vincent Benét

NON AMO TE   119
Martial

FUNEBRIAL REFLECTIONS   120
Ogden Nash

from AN ESSAY ON MAN 121
    Alexander Pope

"MEN SAY THEY KNOW MANY THINGS" 124
    Henry Thoreau

"MAN IS BUT A CASTAWAY" 125
    Clarence Day

from IN MEMORIAM 126
    Alfred, Lord Tennyson

"REMEMBER, THOUGH THE TELESCOPE EXTEND" 127
    George Dillon

EPILOGUE 128
    Herman Melville

PROGRESS 130
    David McCord

from IN MEMORIAM 131
    Alfred, Lord Tennyson

IT ROLLS ON 132
    Morris Bishop

from JOURNAL 133
    Edna St. Vincent Millay

"WHAT AM I, LIFE?" 136
    John Masefield

THE DUNCE 137
    Walter de la Mare

"A MAN SAID TO THE UNIVERSE" 139
    Stephen Crane

HEREDITY 140
    Thomas Hardy

(WITH A DAISY)   141
Emily Dickinson

THE SHAPE OF THE HEART   142
Louise Townsend Nicholl

"SURGEONS MUST BE VERY CAREFUL"   144
Emily Dickinson

THANKSGIVING FOR THE BODY   145
Thomas Traherne

X-RAY   146
Leonora Speyer

THE STAFF OF AESCULAPIUS   147
Marianne Moore

NEW YORK * DECEMBER * 1931   149
Babette Deutsch

from PSALM 8   150

SECTION 4 · Watchers of the Skies

THE SACRED ORDER   155
May Sarton

EPITAPH INTENDED FOR SIR ISAAC NEWTON   157
Alexander Pope

NEWTON   158
William Wordsworth

from TO THE MEMORY OF SIR ISAAC NEWTON   159
James Thomson

"SIR HUMPHRY DAVY"   160
E. C. Bentley

THE FIFTIETH BIRTHDAY OF AGASSIZ   161
   Henry Wadsworth Longfellow

A FAREWELL TO AGASSIZ   163
   Oliver Wendell Holmes

WILLIAM JONES   166
   Edgar Lee Masters

LINES TO DR. DITMARS   167
   Kenneth Allan Robinson

A WELCOME TO DR. BENJAMIN APTHORP GOULD   169
   Oliver Wendell Holmes

RICHARD TOLMAN'S UNIVERSE   171
   Leonard Bacon

THE STAR-SPLITTER   173
   Robert Frost

MR. ATTILA   177
   Carl Sandburg

from GIBBS   178
   Muriel Rukeyser

HOMAGE TO THE PHILOSOPHER   179
   Babette Deutsch

EINSTEIN (1929)   180
   Archibald MacLeish

THE GIFT TO BE SIMPLE   181
   Howard Moss

IN THE EVENING   183
   Thomas Hardy

THE MASTER   185
   C. G. L.

HEART SPECIALIST   186
   Elias Lieberman

LINES WRITTEN AFTER THE DISCOVERY BY
THE AUTHOR OF THE GERM OF YELLOW FEVER   187
   Ronald Ross

A CORRECT COMPASSION   188
   James Kirkup

   INDEX OF AUTHORS   193

   INDEX OF TITLES   195

   INDEX OF FIRST LINES   198

IN THE BEGINNING

IN THE
BEGINNING

The poems in this section are concerned with the creation of the universe, with galaxies, winds, tides, fossils, and shells. Men have always speculated about the beginning of the world, and every civilization has had its own story of creation and its own interpretation of how the sun and moon and stars and earth came to be.

The ancients believed that our earth was the center of the universe and that the sun and moon and stars and planets revolved around it so that man could enjoy the light and warmth of the sun and the beauty of the starry firmament. If we were to believe the evidence of our senses alone we would think exactly as they did, for do we not see that "the sun also arises and goes down and hastes to the place where he arose"? This belief is so universal in human experience that our very language incorporates it in nursery rhymes and everyday sayings.

The doctrine that the sun revolves around the earth found scientific sanction in the works of Ptolemy of Alexandria, a philosopher of the second century A.D. *This Ptolemaic system, as it was called,*

3

was unchallenged for fourteen hundred years, until 1543 when Nicolaus Copernicus' treatise Concerning the Revolution of the Heavenly Bodies *was published. Copernicus, A Polish astronomer who had studied in Italy, remade astronomy, proving by observation and calculation that the earth rotates on its axis and, with the other planets, revolves around the sun. To some this seemed a flat contradiction of Scripture, and it was many years before the "heliocentric theory" gained universal acceptance.*

It may not be too fanciful to suggest that when Shakespeare made Hamlet say, "Doubt that the sun doth move," he may have been aware of these new ideas which the scholars of his time were probably talking about, for ideas then, as now, had a way of floating through the atmosphere. In 1638 John Milton, when he visited Galileo, the most famous of astronomers, may have heard from him an explanation of the cosmic theory that had brought about his partial exile. In Paradise Lost *Milton introduced an exposition of the new astronomy, though he did not accept it fully.*

By the time that Newton's Principia *was published in 1687, and for many years thereafter, there was so much general interest in astronomy and physics that hundreds of poems were written about prisms, optic glasses and the laws of gravitation. By now most of them have been forgotten, but Pope and Thomson, Shelley and Wordsworth remain to us.*

As scientists have found out some of the secrets of nature, poets have added their discoveries to our common experience. These poems are in some part records of scientific achievements; all of them are expressions of wonder at the variousness and beauty of the universe.

4

AUGURIES OF INNOCENCE

To see a World in a grain of sand,
And a Heaven in a wild flower,
Hold Infinity in the palm of your hand,
And Eternity in an hour.

William Blake

from FOUR QUARTETS

We shall not cease from exploration
And the end of all our exploring
Will be to arrive where we started
And know the place for the first time.
Through the unknown, remembered gate
When the last of earth left to discover
Is that which was the beginning;
At the source of the longest river
The voice of the hidden waterfall
And the children in the apple-tree
Not known, because not looked for
But heard, half-heard, in the stillness
Between two waves of the sea.

T. S. Eliot

A VISION

I saw Eternity the other night,
Like a great ring of pure and endless light,
    All calm, as it was bright:—
And round beneath it, Time, in hours, days, years,
    Driven by the spheres,
Like a vast shadow moved; in which the World
    And all her train were hurl'd.

Henry Vaughan

"ATOM FROM ATOM"

Atom from atom yawns as far
As moon from earth, or star from star.

Ralph Waldo Emerson

from "NO SINGLE THING ABIDES"

Sic igitur magni quoque circum moenia mundi
Expugnata dabunt labem putresque ruinas.

I

No single thing abides; but all things flow.
Fragment to fragment clings—the things thus grow
    Until we know and name them. By degrees
They melt, and are no more the things we know.

II

Globed from the atoms falling slow or swift
I see the suns, I see the systems lift
    Their forms; and even the systems and the suns
Shall go back slowly to the eternal drift.

III

Thou too, oh earth—thine empires, lands, and seas—
Least, with thy stars, of all the galaxies,
    Globed from the drift like these, like these thou too
Shalt go. Thou art going, hour by hour, like these.

IV

Nothing abides. Thy seas in delicate haze
Go off; those moonéd sands forsake their place;
    And where they are, shall other seas in turn
Mow with their scythes of whiteness other bays.

9

VIII

Round, angular, soft, brittle, dry, cold, warm,
Things *are* their qualities: things *are* their form—
   And these in combination, even as bees,
Not singly but combined, make up the swarm:

IX

And when the qualities like bees on wing,
Having a moment clustered, cease to cling,
   As the thing dies without its qualities,
So die the qualities without the thing.

X

Where is the coolness when no cool winds blow?
Where is the music when the lute lies low?
   Are not the redness and the red rose one,
And the snow's whiteness one thing with the snow?

XI

Even so, now mark me, here we reach the goal
Of Science, and in little have the whole—
   Even as the redness and the rose are one,
So with the body one thing is the soul.

XIX

The seeds that once were we take flight and fly,
Winnowed to earth, or whirled along the sky,
   Not lost but disunited. Life lives on.
It is the lives, the lives, the lives, that die.

XX

They go beyond recapture and recall,
Lost in the all-indissoluble All:—
    Gone like the rainbow from the fountain's foam,
Gone like the spindrift shuddering down the squall.

XXI

Flakes of the water, on the waters cease!
Soul of the body, melt and sleep like these.
    Atoms to atoms—weariness to rest—
Ashes to ashes—hopes and fears to peace!

XXII

Oh Science, lift aloud thy voice that stills
The pulse of fear, and through the conscience thrills—
    Thrills through the conscience the news of peace—
How beautiful thy feet are on the hills!

Titus Lucretius Carus 95–52 B.C.

Translated by W. H. Mallock

from PROMETHEUS UNBOUND

A sphere, which is as many thousand spheres;
Solid as crystal, yet through all its mass
Flow, as through empty space, music and light;
Ten thousand orbs involving and involved,
Purple and azure, white, green and golden,
Sphere within sphere; and every space between
Peopled with unimaginable shapes,
Such as ghosts dream dwell in the lampless deep;
Yet each inter-transpicuous; and they whirl
Over each other with a thousand motions,
Upon a thousand sightless axles spinning,
And with the force of self-destroying swiftness,
Intensely, slowly, solemnly, roll on,
Kindling with mingled sounds, and many tones,
Intelligible words and music wild.
With mighty whirl the multitudinous orb
Grinds the bright brook into an azure mist
Of elemental subtlety, like light;

．　．　．　．　．

It interpenetrates my granite mass,
　Through tangled roots and trodden clay doth pass
Into the utmost leaves and delicatest flowers;
　Upon the winds, among the clouds 'tis spread,
　It wakes a life in the forgotten dead,
They breathe a spirit up from their obscurest bowers;

．　．　．　．　．

12

Man, oh, not men! a chain of linkèd thought,
  Of love and might to be divided not,
Compelling the elements with adamantine stress;
  As the sun rules even with a tyrant's gaze
  The unquiet republic of the maze
Of Planets, struggling fierce towards heaven's free
    wilderness.

Percy Bysshe Shelley

GENESIS

Chapter 1

In the beginning God created the heaven and the earth.

And the earth was without form, and void; and darkness was upon the face of the deep. And the Spirit of God moved upon the face of the waters.

And God said, Let there be light: and there was light.

And God saw the light, that it was good: and God divided the light from the darkness.

And God called the light Day, and the darkness he called Night. And the evening and the morning were the first day.

And God said, Let there be a firmament in the midst of the waters, and let it divide the waters from the waters.

And God made the firmament, and divided the waters which were under the firmament from the waters which were above the firmament: and it was so.

And God called the firmament Heaven. And the evening and the morning were the second day.

And God said, Let the waters under the heaven be gathered together unto one place, and let the dry land appear: and it was so.

And God called the dry land Earth; and the gathering together of the waters called he Seas: and God saw that it was good.

And God said, Let the earth bring forth grass, the herb yielding seed, and the fruit tree yielding fruit after his kind, whose seed is in itself, upon the earth: and it was so.

And the earth brought forth grass, and herb yielding seed after his kind, and the tree yielding fruit, whose seed was in itself, after his kind: and God saw that it was good.

And the evening and the morning were the third day.

And God said, Let there be lights in the firmament of the heaven to divide the day from the night; and let them be for signs, and for seasons, and for days, and years:

And let them be for lights in the firmament of the heaven to give light upon the earth: and it was so.

And God made two great lights; the greater light to rule the day, and the lesser light to rule the night: he made the stars also.

And God set them in the firmament of the heaven to give light upon the earth,

And to rule over the day and over the night, and to divide the light from the darkness: and God saw that it was good.

And the evening and the morning were the fourth day.

And God said, Let the waters bring forth abundantly the moving creature that hath life, and fowl that may fly above the earth in the open firmament of heaven.

And God created great whales, and every living creature that moveth, which the waters brought forth abundantly, after their kind, and every winged fowl after his kind: and God saw that it was good.

And God blessed them, saying, Be fruitful, and multiply, and fill the waters in the seas, and let fowl multiply in the earth.

And the evening and the morning were the fifth day.

And God said, Let the earth bring forth the living creature after his kind, cattle, and creeping thing, and beast of the earth after his kind: and it was so.

And God made the beast of the earth after his kind, and cattle after their kind, and every thing that creepeth upon the earth after his kind: and God saw that it was good.

And God said, Let us make man in our image, after our likeness: and let them have dominion over the fish of the sea, and over the fowl of the air, and over the cattle, and over all the earth, and over every creeping thing that creepeth upon the earth.

So God created man in his own image, in the image of God created he him; male and female created he them.

And God blessed them, and God said unto them, Be fruitful, and multiply, and replenish the earth, and subdue it: and have dominion over the fish of the sea, and over the fowl of the air, and over every living thing that moveth upon the earth.

And God said, Behold, I have given you every herb bearing seed, which is upon the face of all the earth, and every tree, in the which is the fruit of a tree yielding seed; to you it shall be for meat.

And to every beast of the earth, and to every fowl of the air, and to every thing that creepeth upon the earth, wherein there is life, I have given every green herb for meat: and it was so.

And God saw every thing that he had made, and, behold, it was very good. And the evening and the morning were the sixth day.

"GOD'S FIRST CREATURE WAS LIGHT"

From dark the striped muscles sprang,
The lion mane, the spotted foot.
Across the dark was gently put
The lengthening and hungry fang.

Onto the open firmament,
With each black star a stepping stone,
Fierce, supple, silent and alone,
Light, the first creature, softly went.

Winifred Welles

THE TORTOISE IN ETERNITY

Within my house of patterned horn
I sleep in such a bed
As men may keep before they're born
And after they are dead.

Sticks and stones may break their bones,
And words may make them bleed;
There is not one of them who owns
An armour to his need.

Tougher than hide or lozenged bark,
Snow-storm and thunder proof,
And quick with sun, and thick with dark,
Is this my darling roof.

Men's troubled dreams of death and birth
Pulse mother-o'-pearl to black;
I bear the rainbow bubble Earth
Square on my scornful back.

Elinor Wylie

THE GOD OF GALAXIES

The god of galaxies has more to govern
Than the first men imagined, when one mountain
Trumpeted his anger, and one rainbow,
Red in the east, restored them to his love.
One earth it was, with big and lesser torches,
And stars by night for candles. And he spoke
To single persons, sitting in their tents.

Now streams of worlds, now powdery great whirlwinds
Of universes far enough away
To seem but fog-wisps in a bank of night
So measureless the mind can sicken, trying—
Now seas of darkness, shoreless, on and on
Encircled by themselves, yet washing farther
Than the last triple sun, revolving, shows.

The god of galaxies—how shall we praise him?
For so we must, or wither. Yet what word
Of words? And where to send it, on which night
Of winter stars, of summer, or by autumn
In the first evening of the Pleiades?
The god of galaxies, of burning gases,
May have forgotten Leo and the Bull.

But God remembers, and is everywhere.
He even is the void, where nothing shines.
He is the absence of his own reflection
In the deep gulf; he is the dusky cinder
Of pure fire in its prime; he is the place

Prepared for hugest planets: black idea,
Brooding between fierce poles he keeps apart.

Those altitudes and oceans, though, with islands
Drifting, blown immense as by a wind,
And yet no wind; and not one blazing coast
Where thought could live, could listen—oh, what word
Of words? Let us consider it in terror,
And say it without voice. Praise universes
Numberless. Praise all of them. Praise Him.

Mark Van Doren

ONCE A CHILD

It troubled me as once I was,
For I was once a child,
Deciding how an atom fell
And yet the heavens held.

The heavens weighed the most by far,
Yet blue and solid stood
Without a bolt that I could prove;
Would giants understand?

Life set me larger problems,
Some I shall keep to solve
Till algebra is easier
Or simpler proved above.

Then too be comprehended
What sorer puzzled me,
Why heaven did not break away
And tumble blue on me.

Emily Dickinson

from TROILUS AND CRESSIDA

The heavens themselves, the planets and this center,
Observe degree, priority and place,
Insisture, course, proportion, season, form,
Office and custom, in all line of order:
And therefore is the glorious planet Sol
In noble eminence enthroned and sphered
Amidst the other; whose medicinable eye
Corrects the ill aspects of planets evil,
And posts like the commandment of a king,
Sans check to good and bad: but when the planets
In evil mixture to disorder wander,
What plagues and what portents, what mutiny,
What raging of the sea, shaking of earth,
Commotion in the winds, frights, changes, horrors,
Divert and crack, rend and deracinate
The unity and married calm of states
Quite from their fixture! O, when degree is shaked,
Which is the ladder to all high designs,
The enterprise is sick!

William Shakespeare

from HUDIBRAS

Second Part, Canto III

The Egyptians say, The Sun has twice
Shifted his setting and his rise;
Twice has he risen in the West,
As many times set in the East;
But whether that be true, or no,
The Devil any of you know.
Some hold, the Heavens, like a Top,
Are kept by Circulation up;
And 'twere not for their wheeling round,
They'd instantly fall to the ground:
As sage Empedocles of old,
And from him Modern Authors hold.
Plato believ'd the Sun and Moon,
Below all other Planets run.
Some Mercury, some Venus seat
Above the Sun himself in height.
The learned Scaliger complain'd
'Gainst what Copernicus maintain'd,
That in Twelve hundred years, and odd,
The Sun had left his antient Road,
And nearer to the Earth, is come
'Bove Fifty thousand miles from home.

Samuel Butler

23

MY FATHER'S WATCH

One night I dreamed I was locked in my Father's watch
With Ptolemy and twenty-one ruby stars
Mounted on spheres and the Primum Mobile
Coiled and gleaming to the end of space
And the notched spheres eating each other's rinds
To the last tooth of time, and the case closed.

What dawns and sunsets clattered from the conveyer
Over my head and his while the ruby stars
Whirled rosettes about their golden poles.
"Man, what a show!" I cried. "Infinite order!"
Ptolemy sang. "The miracle of things
Wound endlessly to the first energy
From which all matter quickened and took place!"

"What makes it shine so bright?" I leaned across
Fast between two teeth and touched the mainspring.
At once all hell broke loose. Over our heads
Squadrons of band saws ripped at one another
And broken teeth spewed meteors of flak
From the red stars. You couldn't dream that din:
I broke and ran past something into somewhere
Beyond a glimpse of Ptolemy split open,
And woke on a numbered dial where two black swords
Spun under a crystal dome. There, looking up
In one flash as the two swords closed and came,
I saw my Father's face frown through the glass.

John Ciardi

THIS DIM AND PTOLEMAIC MAN

For forty years, for forty-one,
Sparing the profits of the sun,
This farmer piled his meagre hoard
To buy at last a rattly Ford.

Now crouched on a scared smile he feels
Motion spurt beneath his heels,
Rheumatically intent shifts gears,
Unloosing joints of rustic years.

Morning light obscures the stars,
He swerves avoiding other cars,
Wheels with the road, does not discern
He eastward goes at every turn,

Nor how his aged limbs are hurled
Through all the motions of the world,
How wild past farms, past ricks, past trees,
He perishes toward Hercules.

John Peale Bishop

A DIFFERENT SPEECH

(Associated Press, October 3, 19–)

By special lens, photo-electric cells,
"Rays from the moon were heard throughout Great Bri-
    tain,"
Whose tone was like "the tolling of large bells
Deprived of resonance"; so it was written.

That moonlight was transmutable to sound
Made news for which a different speech is meant;
In poetry again the rays resound,
Language which met and dovetailed the event.

Louise Townsend Nicholl

26

GO FLY A SAUCER

I've seen one flying saucer. Only when
It flew across our sight in 1910
We little thought about the little men.

But let's suppose the little men were there
To cozy such a disc through foreign air:
Connecticut was dark, but didn't scare.

I wonder what they thought of us, and why
They chose the lesser part of Halley's sky,
And went away and let the years go by

Without return? Or did they not get back
To Mars or Venus through the cosmic flak?
At least they vanished, every spaceman Jack.

Now they are with us in the books, in air,
In argument, in hope, in fear, in spare
Reports from men aloft who saw them there.

The day one saucer cracks, the greatest egg
Since dinosaur and dodo shook a leg
Will give new meaning to the prefix *meg.*

Some say the saucers with their little race
Of little men from Littlesphere in space
Have sensed our international disgrace.

27

And when the thing blows over, up, or what,
They'll gladly land and give us all they've got
So Earth shall cease to be a trouble spot.

One fact as old as Chaucer, Saucer Men:
You may be little as a bantam hen,
But Earth has specialized in little men.

David McCord

ODE TO THE HAYDEN PLANETARIUM

Behold within our Hayden Planetarium
More stars than there are fish in the Aquarium,
With many a planet, asteroid and comet
Suspended like the coffin of Mahomet
With Venus and the Pleiadean Seven
Between a platform Earth and ceiling Heaven!

How dear these intimate associations
With scintillating orbs and constellations—
Aldebaran, Adhara, Caph, Canopus,
Arcturus, Castor, Betelgeuse and Propus,
Andromeda, Orion, Sagittarius,
Boötes, Lyra, Cygnus and Aquarius!

Observe them gaily spinning on their axes,—
Their transits, perihelions, parallaxes,
Eclipses, declinations, right ascensions
And other tricks that Dr. Fisher mentions!
Regard the suns in their celestial courses,
The mighty interplay of cosmic forces,
And witness, with devout anticipation,
The drama of the world's annihilation!

Arthur Guiterman

29

FOR THE CONJUNCTION OF TWO PLANETS

We smile at astrological hopes
And leave the sky to expert men
Who do not reckon horoscopes
But painfully extend their ken
In mathematical debate
With slide and photographic plate.

And yet, protest it if we will,
Some corner of the mind retains
The Medieval man who still
Keeps watch upon those starry skeins
And drives us out of doors at night
To gaze at anagrams of light.

Whatever register or law
Is drawn in digits for these two,
Venus and Jupiter keep their awe,
Wardens of brilliance, as they do
Their dual circuit of the west—
The brightest planet and her guest.

Is any light so proudly thrust
From darkness on our lifted faces
A sign of something we can trust,
Or is it that in starry places
We see the things we long to see
In fiery iconography?

Adrienne Cecile Rich

30

THE PLEIADES

Sweet as violets to a weary heart,
Haunting as the lovely names in old tales,
Beloved as a man's own fields, are the Pleiades.

Why is one star loved and not another?
What magic is there in this little cluster
To hold the human spirit from generation to generation?

Yet there they shine, and a smile comes to men's faces,
A tenderness comes to their eyes, and voices grow quiet
Only to name the little stars, the pretty Pleiades.

Elizabeth Coatsworth

URSA MAJOR

Slung between the homely poplars at the end
of the familiar avenue, the Great
Bear in its lighted hammock swings,
like a neglected gate that neither bars admission nor invites,
hangs on the sagging pole its seven-pointed shape.

Drawn with the precision of an unknown problem
solved in the topmost classroom of the empty sky,
it demonstrates upon the inky blackboard of the night's
immeasurable finity the focal point of light.
For though the pointers seem to indicate the pole,
each star looks through us into outer space
from where the sun that burns behind and past us
animates immediately each barren, crystal face
with ravaged brilliance, that our eyes
must lean out into time to catch, and die in seeing.

James Kirkup

from THE PRINCESS

This world was once a fluid haze of light,
Till toward the centre set the starry tides,
And eddied into suns, that wheeling cast
The planets; then the monster, then the man.

Alfred, Lord Tennyson

WEALTH

Who shall tell what did befall,
Far away in time, when once,
Over the lifeless ball,
Hung idle stars and suns?
What god the element obeyed?
Wings of what wind the lichen bore,
Wafting the puny seeds of power,
Which, lodged in rock, the rock abrade?
And well the primal pioneer
Knew the strong task to it assigned,
Patient through Heaven's enormous year
To build in matter home for mind.
From air the creeping centuries drew
The matted thicket low and wide,
This must the leaves of ages strew
The granite slab to clothe and hide,
Ere wheat can wave its golden pride.
What smiths, and in what furnace, rolled
(In dizzy aeons dim and mute
The reeling brain can ill compute)
Copper and iron, lead and gold?
What oldest star the fame can save
Of races perishing to pave
The planet with a floor of lime?
Dust is their pyramid and mole:
Who saw what ferns and palms were pressed
Under the tumbling mountain's breast,
In the safe herbal of the coal?
But when the quarried means were piled,

34

All is waste and worthless, till
Arrives the wise selecting will,
And, out of slime and chaos, Wit
Draws the threads of fair and fit.
Then temples rose, and towns, and marts,
The shop of toil, the hall of arts;
Then flew the sail across the seas
To feed the North from tropic trees;
The storm-wind wove, the torrent span,
Where they were bid, the rivers ran;
New slaves fulfilled the poet's dream,
Galvanic wire, strong-shouldered steam.
Then docks were built, and crops were stored,
And ingots added to the hoard.
But though light-headed man forget,
Remembering Matter pays her debt:
Still, through her motes and masses, draw
Electric thrills and ties of law,
Which bind the strengths of Nature wild
To the conscience of a child.

Ralph Waldo Emerson

ARK OF THE COVENANT

Light has come again and found
The story true that earth is round,
The dawning water vastly curved
Where ocean in its farthest arc
Is separating from the dark.
Now is the mind consoled and served
By steadfast and continuing fact,
Ocean and light the proof, the pact.

Louise Townsend Nicholl

REVOLUTION

West and away the wheels of darkness roll,
   Day's beamy banner up the east is borne,
Spectres and fears, the nightmare and her foal,
   Drown in the golden deluge of the morn.

But over sea and continent from sight
   Safe to the Indies has the earth conveyed
The fast and moon-eclipsing cone of night,
   Her towering foolscap of eternal shade.

See, in mid heaven the sun is mounted; hark,
   The belfries tingle to the noonday chime.
'Tis silent, and the subterranean dark
   Has crossed the nadir, and begins to climb.

A. E. Housman

THE MOTION OF THE EARTH

A day with sky so wide,
So stripped of cloud, so scrubbed, so vacuumed free
Of dust, that you can see
The earth-line as a curve, can watch the blue
Wrap over the edge, looping round and under,
Making you wonder
Whether the dark has anywhere left to hide.
But the world is slipping away; the polished sky
Gives nothing to grip on; clicked from the knuckle
The marble rolls along the gutter of time—
Earth, star and galaxy
Shifting their place in space.
Noon, sunset, clouds, the equably varying weather,
The diffused light, the illusion of blue,
Conceal each hour a different constellation.
All things are new
Over the sun, but we,
Our eyes on our shoes, go staring
At the asphalt, the gravel, the grass at the roadside, the doorstep,
    the doodles of snails, the crochet of mortar and lime,
Seeking the seeming familiar, though every stride
Takes us a thousand miles from where we were before.

Norman Nicholson

JOB

Chapter 38

. . . . .

Where wast thou when I laid the foundations of the earth? declare,
if thou hast understanding.

Who hath laid the measures thereof, if thou knowest? or who
hath stretched the line upon it?

When the morning stars sang together, and all the sons of God
shouted for joy?

. . . . .

Or who shut up the sea with doors, when it brake forth, as if it
had issued out of the womb?

When I made the cloud the garment thereof, and thick darkness
a swaddlingband for it,

And brake up for it my decreed place, and set bars and doors,

And said, Hitherto shalt thou come, but no further: and here shall
thy proud waves be stayed?

Hast thou commanded the morning since thy days; and caused
the dayspring to know his place;

That it might take hold of the ends of the earth, that the wicked
might be shaken out of it?

. . . . .

Hast thou entered into the springs of the sea? or hast thou walked
in the search of the depth?

· · · · ·

Hast thou perceived the breadth of the earth? declare if thou
knowest it all.

Where is the way where light dwelleth? and as for darkness, where
is the place thereof,

· · · · ·

Hast thou entered into the treasures of the snow? or hast thou seen
the treasures of the hail,

· · · · ·

By what way is the light parted, which scattereth the east wind
upon the earth?

Who hath divided a water-course for the overflowing of waters,
or a way for the lightning of thunder;

To cause it to rain on the earth, where no man is; on the wilder-
ness, wherein there is no man;

To satisfy the desolate and waste ground; and to cause the bud
of the tender herb to spring forth?

Hath the rain a father? or who hath begotten the drops of dew?

Out of whose womb came the ice? and the hoary frost of heaven,
who hath gendered it?

· · · · ·

40

Canst thou bind the sweet influences of Pleiades, or loose the
bands of Orion?

Canst thou bring forth Mazzaroth in his season? or canst thou
guide Arcturus with his sons?

Knowest thou the ordinances of heaven? canst thou set the dominion thereof in the earth?

Canst thou lift up thy voice to the clouds, that abundance of
waters may cover thee?

Canst thou send lightnings, that they may go, and say unto thee,
Here we are?

Who hath put wisdom in the inward parts? or who hath given
understanding to the heart?

Who can number the clouds in wisdom? or who can stay the
bottles of heaven,

When the dust groweth into hardness, and the clods cleave fast
together?

. . . . .

from ROCK

There is stone in me that knows stone,
Substance of rock that remembers the unending unending
Simplicity of rest
While scorching suns and ice ages
Pass over rock-face swiftly as days.
In the longest time of all come the rock's changes,
Slowest of all rhythms, the pulsations
That raise from the planet's core the mountain ranges
And weather them down to sand on the sea-floor.

Kathleen Raine

SHELLS

Reaching down arm-deep into bright water
I gathered on white sand under waves
Shells, drifted up on beaches where I alone
Inhabit a finite world of years and days.
I reached my arm down a myriad years
To gather treasure from the yester-millennial sea-floor,
Held in my fingers forms shaped on the day of creation.

Building their beauty in the three dimensions
Over which the world recedes away from us,
And in the fourth, that takes away ourselves
From moment to moment and from year to year
From first to last they remain in their continuous present.
The helix revolves like a timeless thought,
Instantaneous from apex to rim
Like a dance whose figure is limpet or murex, cowrie or golden
    winkle.

They sleep on the ocean floor like humming-tops
Whose music is the mother-of-pearl octave of the rainbow,
Harmonious shells that whisper for ever in our ears,
'The world that you inhabit has not yet been created.'

Kathleen Raine

from WATER

There is a stream that flowed before the first beginning
Of bounding form that circumscribes
Protophyte and protozoon.
The passive permeable sea obeys,
Reflects, rises and falls as forces of moon and wind
Draw this way or that its weight of waves;
But the mutable water holds no trace
Of crest or ripple or whirlpool; the wave breaks,
Scatters in a thousand instantaneous drops
That fall in sphere and ovoid, film-spun bubbles
Upheld in momentary equilibrium of strain and stress
In the ever-changing network woven between stars.

Kathleen Raine

from JOB

Chapter 36

Behold, God is great, and we know him not, neither can the number of his years be searched out.

For he maketh small the drops of water: they pour down rain according to the vapor thereof:

Which the clouds do drop and distil upon man abundantly.

Also can any understand the spreadings of the clouds, or the noise of his tabernacle?

Behold, he spreadeth his light upon it, and covereth the bottom of the sea.

. . . . .

With clouds he covereth the light; and commandeth it not to shine by the cloud that cometh betwixt.

from THE CLOUD

I

I bring fresh showers for the thirsting flowers,
    From the seas and the streams;
I bear light shade for the leaves when laid
    In their noonday dreams.
From my wings are shaken the dews that waken
    The sweet buds every one,
When rocked to rest on their Mother's breast,
    As she dances about the sun.
I wield the flail of the lashing hail,
    And whiten the green plains under,
And then again dissolve it in rain,
    And laugh as I pass in thunder.

II

I sift the snow on the mountains below,
    And their great pines groan aghast;
And all the night 'tis my pillow white,
    While I sleep in the arms of the blast.
Sublime on the towers of my skiey bowers,
    Lightning my pilot sits;
In a cavern under is fettered the thunder,
    It struggles and howls at fits;
Over earth and ocean with gentle motion,
    This pilot is guiding me,
Lured by the love of the Genii that move
    In the depths of the purple sea;
Over the rills and the crags and the hills,
    Over the lakes and the plains,

46

Wherever he dream, under mountain or stream,
  The Spirit he loves remains;
And I all the while bask in Heaven's blue smile,
  Whilst he is dissolving in rains.

III

The sanguine Sunrise, with his meteor eyes,
  And his burning plumes outspread,
Leaps on the back of my sailing rack,
  When the morning star shines dead:
As on the jag of a mountain crag,
  Which an earthquake rocks and swings,
An eagle alit one moment may sit
  In the light of its golden wings.
And when Sunset may breathe, from the lit sea beneath,
  Its ardours of the rest and of love,
And the crimson pall of eve may fall
  From the depth of heaven above,
With wings folded I rest on mine airy nest,
  As still as a brooding dove.

V

I bind the Sun's throne with a burning zone,
  And the moon's with a girdle of pearl;
The volcanoes are dim, and the stars reel and swim,
  When the whirlwinds my banner unfurl.
From cape to cape, with a bridge-like shape,
  Over a torrent sea,
Sunbeam-proof, I hang like a roof;
  The mountains its columns be.
The triumphal arch, through which I march,
  With hurricane, fire, and snow,

When the Powers of the air are chained to my chair,
   Is the million-coloured bow;
The sphere-fire above its soft colors wove,
   While the moist earth was laughing below.

VI

I am the daughter of earth and water,
   And the nursling of the sky:
I pass through the pores of the ocean and shores;
   I change, but I cannot die.
For after the rain, when with never a stain
   The pavilion of heaven is bare,
And the winds and sunbeams with their convex gleams
   Build up the blue dome of air,
I silently laugh at my own cenotaph,
   And out of the caverns of rain,
Like a child from the womb, like a ghost from the tomb,
   I arise and unbuild it again.

Percy Bysshe Shelley

"LOW-ANCHORED CLOUD"

Low-anchored cloud,
Newfoundland air,
Fountain-head and source of rivers,
Dew-cloth, dream drapery,
And napkin spread by fays;
Drifting meadow of the air,
Where bloom the daisied banks and violets,
And in whose fenny labyrinth
The bittern booms and heron wades;
Spirit of lakes and seas and rivers,
Bear only perfumes and the scent
Of healing herbs to just men's fields!

Henry Thoreau

TO A SNOW-FLAKE

What heart could have thought you?—
Past our devisal
(O filigree petal!)
Fashioned so purely,
Fragilely, surely,
From what Paradisal
Imagineless metal,
Too costly for cost?
Who hammered you, wrought you,
From argentine vapor?—
"God was my shaper.
Passing surmisal,
He hammered, He wrought me,
From curled silver vapor
To lust of His mind;
Thou could'st not have thought me!
So purely, so palely,
Tinily, surely,
Mightily, frailly,
Insculped and embossed,
With His hammer of wind,
And His graver of frost."

Francis Thompson

WEATHER WORDS

I know four winds with names like some strange tune:
Chinook, sirocco, khamsin, and monsoon.
Like water over pebbles in Lost Brook:
Sirocco, monsoon, khamsin, and chinook.

David McCord

PHYSICAL GEOGRAPHY

Sudden refreshment came upon the school
When in the tired afternoon we read
Of Rainfall, mountain ranges, watershed.
The whole United States stretched wide and cool.
Geography was dull; this other kind
With gulfs and glaciers, caves, and Rock Formation
In place of Products, People, Population,
Diffused a thrilling vapor through the mind.

There were three creatures—water, land, and air—
Shifting so lightly yet with deep intent
Over the Country and the Continent,
Great creatures moving somber and aware,
Mixing and changing, making something new.
Theirs was the only work that never stops—
More interesting than Industries and Crops—
Creating clouds and sand and snow and dew.

And they could fashion terror when they listed:
New words like "funnel," "vortex," "spiral motion"
Explained the fearful Storms on Plains and Ocean.
Our dreams were sucked up violently and twisted,
The walls and blackboards slowly curved and spun,
There was a revolving speed, a rising core.
This room would not confine us as before
Since cyclones and tornadoes had begun.

Louise Townsend Nicholl

CONTINENT'S END

At the equinox when the earth was veiled in a late rain, wreathed
   with wet poppies, waiting spring,
The ocean swelled for a far storm and beat its boundary, the
   ground-swell shook the beds of granite.

I gazing at the boundaries of granite and spray, the established
   sea-marks, felt behind me
Mountain and plain, the immense breadth of the continent, before me the mass and doubled stretch of water.

I said: You yoke the Aleutian seal-rocks with the lava and coral
   sowings that flower the south,
Over your flood the life that sought the sunrise faces ours that
   has followed the evening star.

The long migrations meet across you and it is nothing to you, you
   have forgotten us, mother.
You were much younger when we crawled out of the womb and
   lay in the sun's eye on the tideline.

It was long and long ago; we have grown proud since then and
   you have grown bitter; life retains
Your mobile soft unquiet strength; and envies hardness, the in-
   solent quietness of stone.

The tides are in our veins, we still mirror the stars, life is your
   child, but there is in me

Older and harder than life and more impartial, the eye that watched before there was an ocean.

That watched you fill your beds out of the condensation of thin vapor and watched you change them,
That saw you soft and violent wear your boundaries down, eat rock, shift places with the continents.

Mother, though my song's measure is like your surf-beat's ancient rhythm I never learned it of you.
Before there was any water there were tides of fire, both our tones flow from the older fountain.

Robinson Jeffers

EPISTLE TO BE LEFT IN THE EARTH

. . . It is colder now,
                there are many stars,
                            we are drifting
North by the Great Bear,
                  the leaves are falling,
The water is stone in the scooped rocks,
                      to southward
Red sun grey air:
           the crows are
Slow on their crooked wings,
                the jays have left us:
Long since we passed the flares of Orion.
Each man believes in his heart he will die.
Many have written last thoughts and last letters.
None know if our deaths are now or forever:
None know if this wandering earth will be found.

We lie down and the snow covers our garments.
I pray you,
        you (if any open this writing)
Make in your mouths the words that were our names.
I will tell you all we have learned,
                I will tell you everything:
The earth is round,
           there are springs under the orchards,
The loam cuts with a blunt knife,
             beware of
Elms in thunder,
           the lights in the sky are stars—

We think they do not see,
>we think also

The trees do not know nor the leaves of the grasses hear us:
The birds too are ignorant.
>Do not listen.

Do not stand at dark in the open windows.
We before you have heard this:
>they are voices:

They are not words at all but the wind rising.
Also none among us has seen God.
(. . . We have thought often
The flaws of sun in the late and driving weather
Pointed to one tree but it was not so.)
As for the nights I warn you the nights are dangerous:
The wind changes at night and the dreams come.

It is very cold,
>there are strange stars near Arcturus,

Voices are crying an unknown name in the sky.

>*Archibald MacLeish*

THE KINGDOM OF NUMBER

THE KINGDOM
OF NUMBER

The world of mathematics and physics, like the world of imagination, is far removed from the tangible and visible; and yet, to the mathematician, as to the poet, this world of pure form has an enduring reality. It is indeed more harmonious than our daily world with its inconsistencies, its violent contrasts, and its undefinable and often insoluble problems. The mathematician, the physicist, and the chemist are concerned with discovering the underlying laws of the universe and with establishing an orderly system of thought.

In this section there are a few of the hundreds of poems that have been written about this world of mathematics where straight lines, points, and circles exist without the intrusion of the irregularities and imperfections that we cannot escape in the world of living creatures. This human striving for perfection led an eighteenth-century poet to speak of arithmetic and geometry as:

> *"Heavenly pair! by whose conspiring aid*
> *The beauteous fabric of the world was made!"*

To many other poets mathematics has seemed divinely inspired and its purity a reflection of heavenly purity. It is no accident

59

that many of these poems are deeply religious or that many theologians have had a profound interest in mathematics and many mathematicians in theology.

It would be impossible to consider the problems of infinity and eternity without wondering about "The First Cause" of the universe; and great mathematicians, though they seem far removed from the rest of humanity, have been not the proudest, but the humblest of men.

Most productive of the sciences in philosophical speculation, mathematics is as well most productive in humor. In what other science are tricks, paradoxes, and dice throwing taken seriously? What other science takes account of the "Absurdum"? Mathematical riddles are perennial; we still ask, "How old is Ann?" There are many joking rhymes about mathematics; even in Mother Goose we have "Multiplication is vexation" and "As I was going to St. Ives." But the humor that springs from mathematics itself is the most delightful of all. If only the schools would include Alice in their mathematical courses how much could we not learn from the Lecturer in Mathematics who described the four branches of Arithmetic as "Ambition, Distraction, Uglification and Derision" and who turned the rules of logic upside down so that he could transport us through the looking glass?

In these poems you will find space-time and quartz crystal clocks, the sublime and the ridiculous; for all these are a part of poetry as they are a part of mathematics.

"SCIENCE IN GOD"

Science in God, is known to be
A Substance, not a Qualitie.

Robert Herrick

from REPLY TO MR. WORDSWORTH

Space-time, our scientists tell us, is impervious.
It neither evades nor refuses. It curves
As a wave will or a flame—whatever's fervent.

Space-time has no beginning and no end.
It has no door where anything can enter.
How break and enter what will only bend?

Archibald MacLeish

THE WHEEL

The wheel's inventor, nameless demigod,
Who first, bending a strong and supple maple tree,
Created this ancient tool, a tool enduring forever;
This lovely circle, carrying at its center a star!

Through Orpheus and through thee, through the lyre and the
    axle,
Space is no longer impassable by heavy marbles,
And we see gliding like water across the sands
The rocks which by their weight had been chained to one spot.

When the earth trembles and there is thunder within
Thou art honored by the chosen chargers of the underworld,
Remembering the chariots which their great strides had drawn
    along;

But how slow was the wheel of the Olympian chariot!
See now the wheel which spins and vanishes, truly burning
With a speed which even thou didst not discover!

Sully-Prudhomme

Translated by William Dock

63

RELATIVITY

There was a young lady named Bright,
Who traveled much faster than light.
    She started one day
    In the relative way,
And returned on the previous night.

Anonymous

APOSTROPHIC NOTES
FROM THE NEW-WORLD PHYSICS

(The universe, according to Sir James Jeans, British scientist, is a system of waves. Space and time and the physical world of substances have no objective reality apart from the mental concepts of them that man creates with his mind. "Thus we can never know the essential nature of anything.")

SWEET READER

Sweet reader, whom I've never seen,
And who, thereby, is non-existent,
To you my thoughts in space careen,
This page not real, myself so distant!
Substantial dear, all unperceived,
For your reality I've grieved!
And Sir James Jeans
Knows what that means.

AH, LOVE

Ah, Love, my dearest and mine own,
So sweetly tangible in pleasance,
How utterly am I alone—
A widower, save in your presence;
The while in space you undulate,
Most cherished and unconscious mate!
And Sir James Jeans
Knows what that means.

GOOD SIR

Good sir who builded us the span
    That seems to bridge the Hudson River,
Suspending from Aldebaran
    My sometimes quite apparent flivver,
        Your postulates were ill-defined
        Did I not keep the bridge in mind!
            As Sir James Jeans
            Most certainly means.

MOST MERCIFUL GOD

Most merciful and loving God
    Who giveth us the will to wonder
If naught save where we tread is sod
    And naught save what we hear is thunder,
        I stoop upon this seeming knee
        In praise of things I know and see.
           For it is my essential nature
           To simulate a grateful creature.
            If Sir James Jeans
            Knows what that means.

E. B. White

FOUR QUARTZ CRYSTAL CLOCKS

There are four vibrators, the world's exactest clocks;
    and these quartz time-pieces that tell
time intervals to other clocks,
    these workless clocks work well;
independently the same, kept in
    the 41° Bell
    Laboratory time

vault. Checked by a comparator with Arlington,
    they punctualize the 'radio,
cinema,' and 'presse,'—a group the
    Giraudoux truth-bureau
of hoped-for accuracy has termed
    'instruments of truth'. We know—
        as Jean Giraudoux says

certain Arabs have not heard—that Napoleon
    is dead; that a quartz prism when
the temperature changes, feels
    the change and that the then
electrified alternate edges
oppositely charged, threaten
    careful timing; so that

this water-clear crystal as the Greeks used to say,
    this 'clear ice' must be kept at the
same coolness. Repetition, with
    the scientist, should be
synonymous with accuracy.

The lemur-student can see
 that an aye-aye is not

an angwan-tíbo, potto, or loris. The sea-
 side burden should not embarrass
the bell-boy with the buoy-ball
 endeavouring to pass
hotel patronesses; nor could a
 practised ear confuse the glass
 eyes for taxidermists

with eye-glasses from the optometrist. And as
 MEridian-7 one-two
one-two gives, each fifteenth second
 in the same voice, the new
data—'The time will be' so and so—
 you realize that 'when you
 hear the signal', you'll be

hearing Jupiter or jour pater, the day god—
 the salvaged son of Father Time—
telling the cannibal Chronos
 (eater of his proxime
newborn progeny) that punctuality
 is not a crime.

Marianne Moore

THE NAKED WORLD

Surrounded by beakers, by strange coils,
By ovens and flasks with twisted necks,
The chemist, fathoming the whims of attractions,
Artfully imposes on them their precise meetings.

He controls their loves, hidden until now,
Discovers and directs their secret affinities,
Unites them and brings about their abrupt divorces,
And purposefully guides their blind destinies.

Teach me then, to read right to the bottom of your alembics,
O sage, who understands these stark forces,
And the inside of the world beyond all color.

Lead me, I pray, into this dark kingdom:
It is toward inward realities that I strive;
Outward forms, too beautiful, beget only sorrows.

Sully-Prudhomme

Translated by William Dock

THE LABORATORY MIDNIGHT

Science is what the world is, earth and water.
And what its seasons do. And what space fountained it.
It is forges hidden underground. It is the dawn's slow salvo.
It is in the closed retort. And it is not yet.

It looks up and counts the Perseids in August,
A fire from nowhere like signals overhead
And it looks for portents, as redmen on a hill,
In the white stream where Altair swims with the Andromedid.

Now you who know what to believe, who have God with you
By desk and bed, blue fire in the stove;
Whom the rains from the northeast alter but perfect
Into new powers, and new pities, and new love;

Go look in lava flows for newer elements,
And dismantle the electric shape of matter like a house;
And weigh the mountains in small sensitive scales;
Break buds; and test the senses of a mouse;

And if you are unpanicked, tell me what you find
On how the sun flies and the snow is spent,
What blasts and bessemers we live in, that dissolve
All the loam loaned to spine and ligament.

Reuel Denney

from RELIQUES

And mathematics, fresh as May,
Will square the circle one bright day.

Edmund Blunden

MATHEMATICS OR THE GIFT OF TONGUES

This is the Word whose breaking heart
With fire restores the speech of men.
It falls upon all troubled thought
In snow-white flakes of love and pain.

There is no speech nor language where
His starry accents do not shine;
All ancient stories flame with Him
In ultimate design.

This is the pattern that shall save
The word and hearts of troubled men.
The Arithmetic God returns,
The Lord of Love returns again.

And all the hearts of all the earth
Are silvery bright with numberings
And their deep fountains sing with mirth,
Music of archangelic things.

The Word which is the marriage rite
When heaven and earth are joined in one,
This is the festival of light,
The wedding of the earth and sun.

All language breathes as does the Bride.
Its innocent splendor brightly burns.
This is the nuptial hour for now
The Arithmetic God returns.

His law goes out to all the earth,
The rhythmic law that once we knew.
This is the old creative power
That builds all things anew.

And all the tongues of all the earth
In which the Names of God are heard
Chant: All shall be as it was made.
In the Beginning was the Word.

He comes with planetary might,
He comes with pentecostal power,
And every heart with deep delight
Unfolds its number like a flower.

'Round His strange bridals of delight
All starry alphabets await.
The Lord of geometric pride
Descends with passion and with state.

And I am changed with his embrace,
My flesh is bright with letterings,
The geometric shapes in which
His algebraic number sings.

I blossom like the Heavenly Rose
In which all words combine to be.
The thousand petals of my names
Dance in a starry ecstasy.

This is the Resurrected Lord
Whose flesh they broke with cruel pain.
The Mathematic Power returns,
The Lord of Love is whole again.

Anna Hempstead Branch

"EUCLID ALONE HAS LOOKED ON BEAUTY BARE"

Euclid alone has looked on Beauty bare.
Let all who prate of Beauty hold their peace,
And lay them prone upon the earth and cease
To ponder on themselves the while they stare
At nothing, intricately drawn nowhere
In shapes of shifting lineage; let geese
Gabble and hiss, but heroes seek release
From dusty bondage into luminous air.
O blinding hour, O holy, terrible day,
When first the shaft into his vision shone
Of light anatomized! Euclid alone
Has looked on Beauty bare. Fortunate they
Who, though once only and then but far away,
Have heard her massive sandal set on stone.

Edna St. Vincent Millay

TULIPS

An age being mathematical, these flowers
Of linear stalks and spheroid blooms were prized
By men with wakened, speculative minds,
And when with mathematics they explored
The Macrocosm, and came at last to
The Vital Spirit of the World, and named it
Invisible Pure Fire, or, say, the Light,
The Tulips were the Light's receptacles.

The gold, the bronze, the red, the bright-swart Tulips!
No emblems they for us who no more dream
Of mathematics burgeoning to light
With Newton's prism and Spinoza's lens,
Or Berkeley's ultimate, Invisible Pure Fire.
In colored state and carven brilliancy
We see them now, or, more illumined,
In sudden fieriness, as flowers fit
To go with vestments red on Pentecost.

Padraic Colum

"TO THINK THAT TWO AND TWO ARE FOUR"

—To think that two and two are four
   And neither five nor three,
The heart of man has long been sore
   And long 'tis like to be.

A. E. Housman

ARITHMETIC

Arithmetic is where numbers fly like pigeons in and out of your head.

Arithmetic tells you how many you lose or win if you know how many you had before you lost or won.

Arithmetic is seven eleven all good children go to heaven—or five six bundle of sticks.

Arithmetic is numbers you squeeze from your head to your hand to your pencil to your paper till you get the answer.

Arithmetic is where the answer is right and everything is nice and you can look out of the window and see the blue sky—or the answer is wrong and you have to start all over and try again and see how it comes out this time.

If you take a number and double it and double it again and then double it a few more times, the number gets bigger and bigger and goes higher and higher and only arithmetic can tell you what the number is when you decide to quit doubling.

Arithmetic is where you have to multiply—and you carry the multiplication table in your head and hope you won't lose it.

If you have two animal crackers, one good and one bad, and you eat one and a striped zebra with streaks all over him eats the other, how many animal crackers will you have if somebody offers you five six seven and you say No no no and you say Nay nay nay and you say Nix nix nix?

If you ask your mother for one fried egg for breakfast and she gives you two fried eggs and you eat both of them, who is better in arithmetic, you or your mother?

Carl Sandburg

78

"THERE WAS AN OLD MAN
WHO SAID, 'DO' "

There was an old man who said, "Do
Tell me *how* I should add two and two?
   I think more and more
   That it makes about four—
But I fear that is almost too few."

Anonymous

"THERE WAS A YOUNG MAN
FROM TRINITY"

There was a young man from Trinity,
Who solved the square root of infinity.
While counting the digits,
He was seized by the fidgets,
Dropped science, and took up divinity.

Anonymous

EUCLID

Old Euclid drew a circle
On a sand-beach long ago,
He bound it and enclosed it
With angles thus and so.
His set of solemn graybeards
Nodded and argued much
Of arc and of circumference,
Diameter and such.
A silent child stood by them
From morning until noon
Because they drew such charming
Round pictures of the moon.

Vachel Lindsay

E = MC²

What was our trust, we trust not,
    What was our faith, we doubt;
Whether we must or not
    We may debate about.
The soul, perhaps, is a gust of gas
    And wrong is a form of right—
But we know that Energy equals Mass
    By the Square of the Speed of Light.

What we have known, we know not,
    What we have proved, abjure.
Life is a tangled bowknot,
    But one thing still is sure.
Come, little lad; come, little lass,
    Your docile creed recite:
"We know that Energy equals Mass
    By the Square of the Speed of Light."

Morris Bishop

THE STARFISH

Triangles are commands of God
   And independent lie
Outside our brains as wild geese show
   Travelling down the sky.

And this five-pointed thing that sucks
   Its slow way as it can
Has as sure a hold on God
   As great Aldebaran.

It has as large a power to please
   Any eye that gazes
Upon its harmony of lines
   As ancient Attic vases.

Pentagon for Gawain's shield,
   Five points of chivalry,
In ancient laws and musical
   It creeps below the sea.

Its fingers are on God's own hand,
   Its just name is a star,
Through aeons it remains as right
   As birth and dying are.

Robert P. Tristram Coffin

THE ICOSASPHERE

'In Buckinghamshire hedgerows
   the birds nesting in the merged green density,
      weave little bits of string and moths and feathers
        and thistledown,
      in parabolic concentric curves'
   and, working for concavity, leave spherical feats
      of rare efficiency;
   whereas through lack of integration,

avid for someone's fortune,
   three were slain and ten committed perjury,
      six died, two killed themselves, and two paid
        fines for risks they'd run.
   But then there is the icosasphere
   in which at last we have steel-cutting at its
      summit of economy,
   since twenty triangles conjoined, can wrap one

ball or double-rounded shell
   with almost no waste, so geometrically
      neat, it's an icosahedron. Would the engineers
        making one,
   or Mr. J. O. Jackson tell us
how the Egyptians could have set up seventy-eight-
      foot solid granite vertically?
We should like to know how that was done.

Marianne Moore

84

from THE PRELUDE

Book VI

'Tis told by one whom stormy waters threw,
With fellow-sufferers by the shipwreck spared,
Upon a desert coast, that having brought
To land a single volume, saved by chance,
A treatise of Geometry, he wont,
Although of food and clothing destitute,
And beyond common wretchedness depressed,
To part from company and take this book
(Then first a self-taught pupil in its truths)
To spots remote, and draw his diagrams
With a long staff upon the sand, and thus
Did oft beguile his sorrow, and almost
Forget his feeling: so (if like effect
From the same cause produced, 'mid outward things
So different, may rightly be compared),
So was it then with me, and so will be
With Poets ever. Mighty is the charm
Of those abstractions to a mind beset
With images and haunted by herself,
And specially delightful unto me
Was that clear synthesis built up aloft
So gracefully; even then when it appeared
Not more than a mere plaything, or a toy
To sense embodied: not the thing it is
In verity, an independent world,
Created out of pure intelligence.

William Wordsworth

85

from HUDIBRAS

First Part, Canto I

In Mathematicks he was greater
Than Tycho Brahe, or Erra Pater:
For he, by Geometrick scale,
Could take the size of Pots of Ale;
Resolve by Signs and Tangents streight,
If Bread or Butter wanted weight;
And wisely tell what hour o' th' day
The Clock doth strike, by Algebra.

Samuel Butler

PLANE GEOMETRY

'Twas Euclid, and the theorem pi
    Did plane and solid in the text,
All parallel were the radii,
    And the ang-gulls convex'd.

"Beware the Wentworth-Smith, my son,
    And the Loci that vacillate;
Beware the Axiom, and shun
    The faithless Postulate."

He took his Waterman in hand;
    Long time the proper proof he sought;
Then rested he by the XYZ
    And sat awhile in thought.

And as in inverse thought he sat
    A brilliant proof, in lines of flame,
All neat and trim, it came to him.
    Tangenting as it came.

"AB, CD," reflected he—
    The Waterman went snicker-snack—
He Q.E.D.-ed, and, proud indeed,
    He trapezoided back.

87

"And hast thou proved the 29th?
    Come to my arms, my radius boy!
O good for you! O one point two!"
    He rhombused in his joy.

'Twas Euclid, and the theorem pi
    Did plane and solid in the text;
All parallel were the radii,
    And the ang-gulls convex'd.

Emma Rounds

"THE POINT, THE LINE, THE SURFACE AND SPHERE"

The point, the line, the surface and sphere,
In seed, stem, leaf, and fruit appear.

Claude Bragdon

ENTROPY

Matter whose movement moves us all
Moves to its random funeral,
And Gresham's law that fits the purse
Seems to fit the universe.
Against the drift what form can move?
(The God of order is called Love.)

Theodore Spencer

from NUMBERS AND FACES

The Kingdom of Number is all boundaries
Which may be beautiful and must be true;
To ask if it is big or small proclaims one
The sort of lover who should stick to faces.

.   .   .   .   .

True, between faces almost any number
Might come in handy, and One is always real;
But which could any face call good, for calling
Infinity a number does not make it one.

W. H. Auden

BOTH MAN AND BIRD AND BEAST

BOTH MAN
AND BIRD
AND BEAST

*The noble words of the Eighth Psalm, "What is man, that thou
art mindful of him?" are an expression of awe and of humbleness,
yet the Psalmist was not troubled by doubts about man's place in
the cosmos.
Just as the earth seemed to the ancient philosophers the center of
the universe, so man seemed the center of all life, the being for
whose benefit all the universe had been created.*

*For many hundreds of years the poets reflected the view that man
is as a being created in God's image, and the scientists did not con-
tradict it. Even though Copernicus had upset the cosmic apple cart,
science during the seventeenth and eighteenth centuries was re-
garded on the whole as beneficent. Then in 1859 Darwin's* Origin
of Species *electrified the listening earth. Edmund Gosse describes
this as "the great moment in the history of thought when the theory
of the mutability of species was preparing to throw a flood of light
upon all departments of human speculation and action." True
enough, the geologist Lyell and Darwin's co-worker Wallace had*

95

foreshadowed this theory, and Darwin's grandfather, Erasmus Darwin, many years before had formulated the beginning of a theory of evolution. It is interesting to recall that an early poem of Tennyson's written long before 1859 defined the evolutionary process in almost Darwinian terms. It was Charles Darwin, though, who first assembled all the facts in an orderly fashion and formed the hypotheses which are the foundation stones of the theory of evolution. On the day of publication, the entire edition of the Origin of Species *was exhausted; the disturbance that followed, like the ever widening ripples caused by a stone thrown into clear water, has not yet subsided.*

To those who believed in a literal interpretation of the first chapter of Genesis, the idea that forms of life had evolved over countless centuries was heresy. The controversy was to affect not only scientists and poets, not only theologians and philosophers, but every man and woman all over the earth. If man was not specially created in God's image what then was he? Was he a descendant of monkeys? (Darwin never made any such statement; his opponents used it for dramatic effect.) Was man a biological accident or sport, who might some day disappear like the dodo and the dinosaur and be replaced by the termite? Was he only a member of the animal kingdom with nothing to distinguish him from the beasts that perish save a few physiological differences in brain and hand structure?

These terrible questions agitated men as never before. As we look back on the Victorian era, so often described as an age of faith, we should be mindful that it was an age of doubt, an age as anxious as our own. Most moving of the poems that express the turmoil of

96

the nineteenth century is Matthew Arnold's "Dover Beach" with its unforgettable close:

> *"And we are here as on a darkling plain*
> *Swept with confused alarms of struggle and flight,*
> *Where ignorant armies clash by night."*

Psalmist and poet, scientist and philosopher have speculated about man's place in the universe. Their struggles are not battles long-ago but are the conflicts that all of us must resolve within ourselves to find our own answer to the Psalmist's question.

"THE FORCE THAT THROUGH THE GREEN FUSE DRIVES THE FLOWER"

The force that through the green fuse drives the flower
Drives my green age; that blasts the roots of trees
Is my destroyer.
And I am dumb to tell the crooked rose
My youth is bent by the same wintry fever.

The force that drives the water through the rocks
Drives my red blood; that dries the mouthing streams
Turns mine to wax.
And I am dumb to mouth unto my veins
How at the mountain spring the same mouth sucks.

The hand that whirls the water in the pool
Stirs the quicksand; that ropes the blowing wind
Hauls my shroud sail.
And I am dumb to tell the hanging man
How of my clay is made the hangman's lime.

The lips of time leech to the fountain head;
Love drips and gathers, but the fallen blood
Shall calm her sores.
And I am dumb to tell a weather's wind
How time has ticked a heaven round the stars.

And I am dumb to tell the lover's tomb
How at my sheet goes the same crooked worm.

Dylan Thomas

MESSAGE FROM HOME

Do you remember, when you were first a child,
Nothing in the world seemed strange to you?
You perceived, for the first time, shapes already familiar,
And seeing, you knew that you had always known
The lichen on the rock, fern-leaves, the flowers of thyme,
As if the elements newly met in your body,
Caught up into the momentary vortex of your living
Still kept the knowledge of a former state,
In you retained recollection of cloud and ocean,
The branching tree, the dancing flame.

Now when nature's darkness seems strange to you,
And you walk, an alien, in the streets of cities,
Remember earth breathed you into her with the air, with the
    sun's rays,
Laid you in her waters asleep, to dream
With the brown trout among the milfoil roots,
From substance of star and ocean fashioned you,
At the same source conceived you
As sun and foliage, fish and stream.

Of all created things the source is one,
Simple, single as love; remember
The cell and seed of life, the sphere
That is, of child, white bird, and small blue dragon-fly
Green fern, and the gold four-petalled tormentilla
The ultimate memory.
Each latent cell puts out a future,
Unfolds its differing complexity

As a tree puts forth leaves, and spins a fate
Fern-traced, bird-feathered, or fish-scaled.
Moss spreads its green film on the moist peat,
The germ of dragon-fly pulses into animation and takes
    wing
As the water-lily from the mud ascends on its ropy stem
To open a sweet white calyx to the sky.
Man, with farther to travel from his simplicity,
From the archaic moss, fish, and lily parts,
And into exile travels his long way.

As you leave Eden behind you, remember your home,
For as you remember back into your own being
You will not be alone; the first to greet you
Will be those children playing by the burn,
The otters will swim up to you in the bay,
The wild deer on the moor will run beside you.
Recollect more deeply, and the birds will come,
Fish rise to meet you in their silver shoals,
And darker, stranger, more mysterious lives
Will throng about you at the source
Where the tree's deepest roots drink from the abyss.

Nothing in that abyss is alien to you.
Sleep at the tree's root, where the night is spun
Into the stuff of worlds, listen to the winds,
The tides, and the night's harmonies, and know
All that you knew before you began to forget,
Before you became estranged from your own being,
Before you had too long parted from those other
More simple children, who have stayed at home
In meadow and island and forest, in sea and river.

Earth sends a mother's love after her exiled son,
Entrusting her message to the light and the air,
The wind and waves that carry your ship, the rain that falls,
The birds that call to you, and all the shoals
That swim in the natal waters of her ocean.

Kathleen Raine

IF THEY SPOKE

The animals will never know;
Could not find out; would scarcely care
That all their names are in our books,
And all their images drawn bare.

What names? They have not heard the sound,
Nor in their silence thought the thing.
They are not notified they live;
Nor ask who set them wandering.

Simply they are. And so with us;
And they would say it if they spoke;
And we might listen; and the world
Be uncreated at one stroke.

Mark Van Doren

COLD-BLOODED CREATURES

Man, the egregious egoist
(In mystery the twig is bent),
Imagines, by some mental twist,
That he alone is sentient

Of the intolerable load
Which on all living creatures lies,
Nor stoops to pity in the toad
The speechless sorrow of its eyes.

He asks no questions of the snake,
Nor plumbs the phosphorescent gloom
Where lidless fishes, broad awake,
Swim staring at a night-mare doom.

Elinor Wylie

INNATE HELIUM

Religious faith is a most filling vapor.
It swirls occluded in us under tight
Compression to uplift us out of weight—
As in those buoyant bird bones thin as paper,
To give them still more buoyancy in flight.
Some gas like helium must be innate.

Robert Frost

THE MASKED SHREW

. . . the masked shrew . . . dies of old age after only about
*a year of fast-paced gluttonous life.—*Life.

A penny is heavier than the shrew.
Dim-eyed, and weaker than a worm,
this smallest mammal, cannoned by a
   sudden noise,
lies down and dies.
No furnace gluttons fiercer than the shrew,
devouring daily with relentless appetite
four times her inchling body's weight.
More extravagant than the humming-bird's, the
   shrew's
heart beats per minute twice four hundred times.
If foodless for six hours, she is dead.
The helpless, hungry, nervous shrew
lives for a year of hurly-burly
and dies intolerably early.

Isabella Gardner

"I SAW A PEACOCK"

I saw a peacock with a fiery tail
I saw a blazing comet drop down hail
I saw a cloud wrapped with ivy round
I saw an oak creep on along the ground
I saw a pismire swallow up a whale
I saw the sea brim full of ale
I saw a Venice glass five fathoms deep
I saw a well full of men's tears that weep
I saw red eyes all of a flaming fire
I saw a house bigger than the moon and higher
I saw the sunset at twelve o'clock at night
I saw the man that saw this wondrous sight.

Anonymous

"OUR LITTLE KINSMEN"

Our little kinsmen after rain
In plenty may be seen,
A pink and pulpy multitude
The tepid ground upon;

A needless life it seemed to me
Until a little bird
As to a hospitality
Advanced and breakfasted.

As I of he, so God of me,
I pondered, may have judged,
And left the little angleworm
With modesties enlarged.

Emily Dickinson

107

THE SPIDER

With six small diamonds for his eyes
He walks upon the Summer skies,
Drawing from his silken blouse
The lacework of his dwelling house.

He lays his staircase as he goes
Under his eight thoughtful toes
And grows with the concentric flower
Of his shadowless, thin bower.

His back legs are a pair of hands,
They can spindle out the strands
Of a thread that is so small
It stops the sunlight not at all.

He spins himself to threads of dew
Which will harden soon into
Lines that cut like slender knives
Across the insects' airy lives.

He makes no motion but is right,
He spreads out his appetite
Into a network, twist on twist,
This little ancient scientist.

He does not know he is unkind,
He has a jewel for a mind
And logic deadly as dry bone,
This small son of Euclid's own.

Robert P. Tristram Coffin

from THE TRIUMPH OF THE WHALE

Io! Paean! Io! sing
To the finny people's King.
Not a mightier Whale than this
In the vast Atlantic is;
Not a fatter fish than he
Flounders round the polar sea.
See his blubber—at his gills
What a world of drink he swills,
From his trunk, as from a spout,
Which next moment he pours out.

. . . .

Name or title, what has he?
Is he Regent of the Sea?
From this difficulty free us,
Buffon, Banks, or sage Linnaeus.
With his wondrous attributes
Say, what appellation suits?
By his bulk, and by his size,
By his oily qualities,
This (or else my eyesight fails),
This should be the Prince of Whales.

Charles Lamb

110

VARIATION ON A SENTENCE

There are few or no bluish animals. . . .
THOREAU'S JOURNALS, FEB. 21, 1855

Of white and tawny, black as ink,
Yellow, and undefined, and pink,
And piebald, there are droves, I think.

(Buff kine in herd, gray whales in pod,
Brown woodchucks, colored like the sod,
All creatures from the hand of God.)

And many of a hellish hue;
But, for some reason hard to view,
Earth's bluish animals are few.

Louise Bogan

THE DINOSAUR

Behold the mighty dinosaur
Famous in prehistoric lore,
Not only for his weight and length
But for his intellectual strength.
You will observe by these remains
The creature had two sets of brains—
One on his head (the usual place),
The other at his spinal base.
Thus he could reason "a priori"
As well as a "a posteriori."
No problem bothered him a bit:
He made both head and tail of it.
So wise he was, so wise and solemn
Each thought filled just a spinal column.
If one brain found the pressure strong
It passed a few ideas along;
If something slipped his forward mind
'Twas rescued by the one behind.
And if in error he was caught
He had a saving afterthought,
As he thought twice before he spoke
He had no judgments to revoke;
For he could think without congestion,
Upon both sides of every question.

Bert Leston Taylor

AT WOODWARD'S GARDENS

A boy, presuming on his intellect,
Once showed two little monkeys in a cage
A burning-glass they could not understand
And never could be made to understand.
Words are no good: to say it was a lens
For gathering solar rays would not have helped.
But let him show them how the weapon worked.
He made the sun a pin-point on the nose
Of first one then the other till it brought
A look of puzzled dimness to their eyes
That blinking could not seem to blink away.
They stood arms laced together at the bars,
And exchanged troubled glances over life.
One put a thoughtful hand up to his nose
As if reminded—or as if perhaps
Within a million years of an idea.
He got his purple little knuckles stung.
The already known had once more been confirmed
By psychological experiment,
And that were all the finding to announce
Had the boy not presumed too close and long.
There was a sudden flash of arm, a snatch,
And the glass was the monkeys' not the boy's.
Precipitately they retired back cage
And instituted an investigation
On their part, though without the needed insight.
They bit the glass and listened for the flavor.
They broke the handle and the binding off it.

Then none the wiser, frankly gave it up,
And having hid it in their bedding straw
Against the day of prisoners' ennui,
Came dryly forward to the bars again
To answer for themselves: Who said it mattered
What monkeys did or didn't understand?
They might not understand a burning-glass.
They might not understand the sun itself.
It's knowing what to do with things that counts.

Robert Frost

METROPOLITAN NIGHTMARE

It rained quite a lot, that spring. You woke in the morning
And saw the sky still clouded, the streets still wet,
But nobody noticed so much, except the taxis
And the people who parade. You don't in a city.
The parks got very green. All the trees were green
Far into July and August, heavy with leaf,
Heavy with leaf and the long roots boring and spreading,
But nobody noticed that but the city gardeners,
And they don't talk.

                  Oh, on Sundays, perhaps, you'd notice:
Walking through certain blocks, by the shut, proud houses
With the windows boarded, the people gone away,
You'd suddenly see the queerest small shoots of green
Poking through cracks and crevices in the stone
And a bird-sown flower, red on a balcony,
But then you made jokes about grass growing in the streets
And the end of the depression—and there were songs
And gags and a musical show called "Hot and Wet."
It all made a good box for the papers. When the flamingo
Flew into a meeting of the Board of Estimate,
Mayor O'Brien acted at once and called the photographers.
When the first green creeper crawled upon Brooklyn Bridge,
They thought it was ornamental. They let it stay.

That was the year the termites came to New York
And they don't do well in cold climates—but listen, Joe,
They're only ants and ants are nothing but insects.

It was funny and yet rather wistful, in a way
(As Heywood Broun pointed out in the *World-Telegram*),
To think of them looking for wood in a steel city.
It made you feel about life. It was too divine.
There were funny pictures by Steig and Peter Arno
And Macy's ran a terribly clever ad:
"The Widow's Termite" or something.

                                   There was no
Disturbance. Even the Communists didn't protest
And say they were Morgan hirelings. It was too hot,
Too hot to protest, too hot to get excited,
An even, African heat, lush, fertile, and steamy,
That soaked into bone and mind and never once broke.
The warm rain fell in fierce showers and ceased and fell.
Pretty soon you got used to its always being that way.

You got used to the changed rhythm, the altered beat,
To people walking slower, to the whole bright
Fierce pulse of the city slowing, to men in shorts,
The new sun helmets from Best's and cops' white uniforms
And the long noon rest in the offices, everywhere.

It wasn't a plan or anything. It just happened.
The fingers tapped the keys slower, the office boys
Dozed on their benches, the bookkeeper yawned at his desk.
The A.T.&T. was the first to change the shifts
And establish an official siesta-room,
But they were always efficient. Mostly it just
Happened like sleep itself, like a tropic sleep,
Till even the Thirties were deserted at noon

116

Except for a few tourists and one damp cop.
They ran boats to see the lilies on the North River,
But it was only the tourists who really noticed
The flocks of rose-and-green parrots and parakeets
Nesting in the stone crannies of the Cathedral.
The rest of us had forgotten when they first came.

There wasn't any real change, it was just a heat spell,
A rain spell, a funny summer, a weatherman's joke
In spite of the geraniums three feet high
In the tin-can gardens of Hester and Desbrosses.
New York was New York. It couldn't turn inside out.
When they got the news from Woods Hole about the Gulf
    Stream,
The *Times* ran an adequate story,
But nobody reads those stories but science cranks.

Until, one day, a somnolent city editor
Gave a new cub the termite yarn to break his teeth on.
The cub was just down from Vermont, so he took the time.
He was serious about it. He went around.
He read all about termites in the Public Library
And it made him sore when they fired him.
                              So, one evening,
Talking with an old watchman, beside the first
Raw girders of the new Planetopolis Building
(Ten thousand brine-cooled offices, each with shower),
He saw a dark line creeping across the rubble
And turned a flashlight on it.
                    "Say, buddy," he said.

117

"You better look out for those ants. They eat wood, you know.
They'll have your shack down in no time."

                                                  The watchman spat.
"Oh, they've quit eating wood," he said, in a casual voice.
"I thought everybody knew that."

                                              —and, reaching down,
He pried from the insect jaws the bright crumb of steel.

Stephen Vincent Benét

118

NON AMO TE

I do not love thee, Doctor Fell,
The reason why I cannot tell;
But this I know, and know full well,
I do not love thee, Doctor Fell.

Martial

Translated by Thomas Brown

FUNEBRIAL REFLECTIONS

Among the anthropophagi
People's friends are people's sarcophagi.

Ogden Nash

from AN ESSAY ON MAN

Far as creation's ample range extends,
The scale of sensual, mental powers ascends.
Mark how it mounts, to man's imperial race,
From the green myriads in the peopled grass.
What modes of sight betwixt each wide extreme:
The mole's dim curtain and the lynx's beam;
Of smell, the headlong lioness between,
And hound sagacious on the tainted green;
Of hearing, from the life that fills the flood,
To that which warbles thro' the vernal wood;
The spider's touch, how exquisitely fine!
Feels at each thread and lives along the line;
In the nice bee, what sense so subtly true
From pois'nous herbs extracts the healing dew?
How instinct varies in the grov'lling swine,
Compared, half-reas'ning elephant, with thine!
'Twixt that, and reason, what a nice barrier,
Forever sep'rate, yet forever near!
Remembrance and reflection how allied,
What thin partitions sense from thought divide;
And middle natures, how they long to join,
Yet never pass th' insuperable line!
Without this just gradation, could they be
Subjected, these to those, or all to thee?
The pow'rs of all subdued by thee alone—
Is not thy reason all these pow'rs in one?

See thro' this air, this ocean, and this earth
All matter quick and bursting into birth:
Above, how high progressive life may go!
Around, how wide! how deep extend below!
Vast chain of being! which from God began,
Nature's ethereal, human, angel, man;
Beast, bird, fish, insect, what no eye can see,
No glass can reach—from Infinite to thee,
From thee to nothing.

EPISTLE II

Know then thyself, presume not God to scan,
The proper study of mankind is Man.
Placed on this isthmus of a middle state,
A being darkly wise, and rudely great:

. . . . .

Created half to rise, and half to fall;
Great lord of all things, yet a prey to all;
Sole judge of truth, in endless error hurled;
The glory, jest, and riddle of the world!
Go, wondrous creature! mount where science guides:
Go, measure earth, weigh air, and state the tides:
Instruct the planets in what orbs to run,
Correct old time and regulate the Sun;
Go, soar with Plato to th' empyreal sphere,
To the first good, first perfect, and first fair;
Or tread the mazy round his follow'rs trod
And quitting sense call imitating God—
As Eastern priests in giddy circles run,

And turn their heads to imitate the Sun.
Go, teach Eternal Wisdom how to rule:
Then drop into thyself, and be a fool!
   Superior beings, when of late they saw
A mortal man unfold all nature's law,
Admired such wisdom in an earthly shape,
And showed a NEWTON as we show an ape.
   Could he, whose rules the rapid comet bind,
Describe or fix one movement of his mind?
Who saw its fires here rise and there descend,
Explain his own beginning or his end?
Alas, what wonder: man's superior part
Unchecked may rise, and climb from art to art,
But when his own great work is but begun,
What reason weaves by passion is undone.

Alexander Pope

"MEN SAY THEY KNOW MANY THINGS"

Men say they know many things;
But lo! they have taken wings,—
The arts and sciences,

And a thousand appliances;
The wind that blows
Is all that any body knows.

Henry Thoreau

"MAN IS BUT A CASTAWAY"

Man is but a castaway
    On this planet's shore.
He survives from day to day.
    Can he ask for more?
Vast and intricate the store
    Of his printed words.
Short and simple is the lore
    Of the beasts and birds.

Clarence Day

from IN MEMORIAM

And, star and system rolling past,
A soul shall draw from out the vast
And strike his being into bounds,

And moved thro' life of lower phase,
Result in man, be born and think,
And act and love, a closer link
Betwixt us and the crowning race

Of those that, eye to eye, shall look
On knowledge; under whose command
Is Earth and Earth's, and in their hand
Is Nature like an open book;

No longer half-akin to brute,
For all we thought and loved and did,
And hoped, and suffer'd, is but seed
Of what in them is flower and fruit;

Whereof the man that with me trod
This planet was a noble type
Appearing ere the times were ripe,
That friend of mine who lives in God,

That God, which ever lives and loves,
One God, one law, one element,
And one far-off divine event,
To which the whole creation moves.

Alfred, Lord Tennyson

126

"REMEMBER,
THOUGH THE TELESCOPE EXTEND"

Remember, though the telescope extend
Few manifestoes Time may not efface
When earth has wandered to her freezing end
And left no footprint on the paths of space,
How of all living creatures, you alone
Surmise exclusion from the secret plan—
You, with the cipher cut into your own
Most unimaginable substance, Man.
Afraid! Afraid! Yet the bright skies you fear
Were black as doom, were but the want of skies,
Were nothing at all until you happened here,
Bearing the little lanterns of your eyes.
In the first gathering of the ultimate frost
Remember this and let the world be lost.

George Dillon

EPILOGUE

If Luther's day expand to Darwin's year,
Shall that exclude the hope—foreclose the fear? . . ,

Yea, ape and angel, strife and old debate—
The harps of heaven and dreary gongs of hell;
Science the feud can only aggravate—
No umpire she betwixt the chimes and knell:
The running battle of the star and clod
Shall run for ever—if there be no God.

Degrees we know, unknown in days before;
The light is greater, hence the shadow more;
And tantalised and apprehensive Man
Appealing—wherefore ripen us to pain?
Seems there the spokesman of dumb Nature's train.

But through such strange illusions have they passed
Who in life's pilgrimage have baffled striven—
Even death may prove unreal at the last,
And stoics be astounded into heaven.

Then keep thy heart, though yet but ill-resigned—
Clarel, thy heart, the issues there but mind;
That like the crocus budding through the snow—
That like a swimmer rising from the deep—

That like a burning secret which doth go
Even from the bosom that would hoard and keep;
Emerge thou mayst from the last whelming sea,
And prove that death but routs life into victory.

Herman Melville

PROGRESS

Darwin and Mendel laid on man the chains
That bind him to the past. Ancestral gains,
So pleasant for a spell, of late bizarre,
Suggest that where he was is where we are.

David McCord

from IN MEMORIAM

I trust I have not wasted breath:
    I think we are not wholly brain,
    Magnetic mockeries; not in vain,
Like Paul with beasts, I fought with Death;

Not only cunning casts in clay:
    Let Science prove we are, and then
    What matters Science unto men,
At least to me? I would not stay.

Let him, the wiser man who springs
    Hereafter, up from childhood shape
    His action like the greater ape,
But I was *born* to other things.

Alfred, Lord Tennyson

IT ROLLS ON

This is the time of wonder, it is written;
    Man has undone the ultimate mysteries.
      (We turn from the Chrysler Tower to watch a kitten,
    Turn to a dead fish from Isocrates;
Drinkers on five day boats are gladly smitten
    Unconscious on the subjugated seas;
      Einstein is even more dull than Bulwer-Lytton;
    You cannot smoke on the *Los Angeles.*)
Science no longer knows the verb-form "can't."
    Fresh meat will soon be shipped by radio;
    Scholars are harnessing the urgent ant
And making monstrous bastard fruits to grow,
    Building machines for things I do not want,
    Discovering truths I do not care to know.

Morris Bishop

from JOURNAL

I read with varying degrees
Of bile the sage philosophies,
Since not a man has wit to purge
His pages of the Vital Urge.
At my head when I was young
Was Monad of all Monads flung;
And in my ears like any wind
Dubito Ergo Sum was dinned.
(When a chair was not a chair
Was when nobody else was there;
And Bergson's lump of sugar awed
My soul to see how slow it thawed!)

I, too, have mused upon the way
The sun comes up and makes the day,
The tide goes out and makes the shore,
And many, many matters more;
And coaxed till I was out of breath
My mind to take the hurdle, Death.
I, too, have writ my little book
On Things 'Twere Best to Overlook;
And struck a match and drawn a cork
And called a spade a salad-fork.
For men that are afraid to die
Must warm their hands before a lie;
The fire that's built of What is Known
Will chill the marrow in the bone.

Listen to a little story:
One day in a laboratory,
Where I was set to guess and grope,
I looked into a microscope.
I saw in perfect pattern sprawl
Something that was not there at all,
Something, perhaps, being utterly
Invisible to the naked eye,
By Descartes' doubt as all untrod
As furrows in the brain of God.
If, now, the naked eye can see
So little of the chemistry
By which itself is hale or blind,—
What, then, about the naked mind?

Think you a brain like as two peas
To any chattering chimpanzee's,
As 'twere a nut in the cheek shall nurse
The riddle of the universe?

Have we no patience, pray, to wait
Until that somewhat out-of-date,
Unwieldy instrument, the mind,
Shall be re-modeled and refined?
Or must we still abuse and vex
Our darkness with the Vital X,
Straining, with nothing given, to scan
The old equation: What is Man?

The sage philosopher at night,
When other men are breathing light,

Out of a troubled sleep I see
Start up in bed, holding the key!—
And wrap him in his dressing-gown,
And get him up and set him down,
And write enough to ease his head,
And rub his hands, and go to bed;—
And at the window, peering through,
All this time—the Bugaboo!

Edna St. Vincent Millay

"WHAT AM I, LIFE?"

What am I, Life? A thing of watery salt
Held in cohesion by unresting cells,
Which work they know not why, which never halt,
Myself unwitting where their Master dwells.
I do not bid them, yet they toil, they spin;
A world which uses me as I use them,
Nor do I know which end or which begin
Nor which to praise, which pamper, which condemn.
So, like a marvel in a marvel set,
I answer to the vast, as wave by wave
The sea of air goes over, dry or wet,
Or the full moon comes swimming from her cave,
Or the great sun comes north, this myriad I
Tingles, not knowing how, yet wondering why.

John Masefield

THE DUNCE

And 'Science' said,
'Attention, Child, to me!
Have I not taught you all
You touch; taste; hear; and see?

'Nought that's true knowledge now
In print is pent
Which my sole method
Did not circumvent.

'Think you, the amoeba
In its primal slime
Wasted on dreams
Its destiny sublime?

'Yet, when I bid
Your eyes survey the board
Whereon life's How, When, Where
I now record,

'I find them fixed
In daydream; and you sigh;
Or, like a silly sheep,
You bleat me, *Why?*

' "Why is the grass so cool, and fresh, and green?
The sky so deep, and blue?"
Get to your Chemistry,
You dullard, you!

' "Why must I sit at books, and learn, and learn,
Yet long to play?"
Where's your Psychology,
You popinjay?

' "Why stay I here,
Not where my heart would be?"
Wait, dunce, and ask that
Of Philosophy!

'Reason is yours
Wherewith to con your task;
Not that unanswerable
Questions you should ask.

'Stretch out your hands, then—
Grubby, shallow bowl—
And be refreshed, Child—
Mind, and, maybe, soul!

'Then—when you grow into
A man—like me;
You will as learnèd, wise,
And—happy be!'

Walter de la Mare

"A MAN SAID TO THE UNIVERSE"

A man said to the universe:
"Sir, I exist!"
"However," replied the universe,
"The fact has not created in me
A sense of obligation."

Stephen Crane

HEREDITY

I am the family face;
Flesh perishes, I live on,
Projecting trait and trace
Through time to times anon,
And leaping from place to place
Over oblivion.

The years-heired feature that can
In curve and voice and eye
Despise the human span
Of durance—that is I;
The eternal thing in man,
That heeds no call to die.

Thomas Hardy

(WITH A DAISY)

A science—so the savants say,
"Comparative Anatomy,"
By which a single bone
Is made a secret to unfold
Of some rare tenant of the mold
Else perished in the stone.
So to the eye prospective led
This meekest flower of the mead,
Upon a winter's day,
Stands representative in gold
Of rose and lily, marigold
And countless butterfly!

Emily Dickinson

THE SHAPE OF THE HEART

The shape of the heart is an old design
Which designates humanity.
Cut from the circle, the Divine,
Its surging wings acutely join
In quick converging symmetry
To make with double curve and quoin
A timeless vase of classic line,
The vessel of mortality.

All contours patterned on the heart,
As lilac leaf, its counterpart,
Do emulate and copy fair
Its guardianship and long persistence.
By any sunken homestead corner
One lilac bush remains, a mourner,
The quiet leaf shaped like a locket
Laid on the breast of dreaming thicket,
A keepsake of a lost existence
Which still is substance of the air.

The hidden heart, the actual urn,
The leaf high in the body's tree,
Has for its ceaseless deep concern
The urgent tides of human ocean
And offers double constancy—
To life itself and its emotion.
The tracing here is not exact:

Expanded, un-identical,
It keeps an unrelenting pact
With atrium and ventricle—
A bell hung pulsing in a tower,
Shape of the mystery, the power.
The static figure of devotion
Now chambered for intensity
Toward early circle makes return,
The rondure of immensity.

Louise Townsend Nicholl

"SURGEONS MUST BE VERY CAREFUL"

Surgeons must be very careful
When they take the knife!
Underneath their fine incisions
Stirs the culprit,—Life!

Emily Dickinson

THANKSGIVING FOR THE BODY

O Lord!
Thou hast given me a body,
Wherein the glory of Thy power shineth,
Wonderfully composed above the beasts,
Within distinguished into useful parts,
Beautified without with many ornaments.
Limbs rarely poised,
And made for Heaven:
Arteries filled
With celestial spirits:
Veins wherein blood floweth,
Refreshing all my flesh,
Like rivers:
Sinews fraught with the mystery
Of wonderful strength,
Stability,
Feeling.
O blessèd be Thy glorious Name!
That thou hast made it
A treasury of Wonders,
Fit for its several Ages;
For Dissections,
For Sculptures in Brass,
For Draughts in Anatomy,
For the contemplation of the Sages.

Thomas Traherne

145

X-RAY

I looked into my body—
Lurking and shadowy there
The building of my bones
Where I had dwelt so long,
So sturdily, so long,
The dreams and griefs among,
Paying no rent at all . . .

And cried, God bless my home!
God bless the builder too
Of each frail, faltering wall,
Essential masonry,
And strong (I thought),
And strong.

God bless the Architect!
(And thought, can one bless God?
Dare bless?—And answered, yes!)
The wise man at my side,
Explaining, did not see
All that was vouchsafed me:
Into that house of bone
I entered—and alone.

Leonora Speyer

THE STAFF OF AESCULAPIUS

A symbol from the first, of mastery,
   experiments such as Hippocrates made
     and substituted for vague
  speculation, stayed
    the ravages of a plague.

A "going on": yes, *anastasis* is the word
   for research a virus has defied,
     and the virologist
  with variables still untried—
    too impassioned to desist.

Suppose that research has hit on the right one
   and a killed vaccine is effective
     say temporarily—
  for even a year—although a live
    one could give lifelong immunity,

knowledge has been gained for another attack.
   Selective injury to cancer
     cells without injury to
  normal ones—another
    gain—looks like prophecy come true.

Now, after lung resection, the surgeon fills space.
   To sponge implanted, cells following
      fluid, adhere and what
   was inert becomes living—
      that was framework. Is it not

like the master-physician's Sumerian rod?
   staff and effigy of the animal
      which by shedding its skin
   is a sign of renewal—
      the symbol of medicine.

Marianne Moore

NEW YORK * DECEMBER * 1931

The child's cough scratches at my heart—my head
Buzzes with rumors of war, appalling news
From China, and queer stories of men bred
In ant-hills which will overthrow the world.
Machines can split the atom, if you choose,
And hens turn into cocks, I have heard said.
This does not unsteady my pulses.
Thoughts are hurled
East, west, and up and down the universe,
But none so dizzying as the sitting still,
In lamplight, among friends
(The cough's not worse?),
And watching eyes beam, lips move, fingers drill
Gently upon the table . . .
Oh, clever, oh, kind!
Here time undoes itself, here we rehearse
A drama not debated by the mind,
And see in fair beginnings fairer ends.
Say children cry, with reason, and men die,
Unreasonably, say our hearts are torn
And our brains puzzled—miracles persist!
Not the halved atom nor the changeling bird,
But this, the dazzling moment, close and human,
That for long pain makes brief complete amends.

Babette Deutsch

from PSALM 8

. . . .

When I consider thy heavens, the work of thy fingers, the moon
and the stars, which thou hast ordained:

What is man, that thou art mindful of him? and the son of man.
that thou visitest him?

For thou hast made him a little lower than the angels, and hast
crowned him with glory and honour.

Thou madest him to have dominion over the works of thy hands;
thou hast put all things under his feet:

All sheep and oxen, yea, and the beasts of the field;

The fowl of the air, and the fish of the sea, and whatsoever
passeth through the paths of the seas.

. . . .

WATCHERS OF THE SKIES

WATCHERS
OF THE SKIES

Though we speak of "science and poetry," these abstractions are meaningless unless we think of them in human terms. Science and poetry are made by scientists and poets; often a scientist expresses himself in the language that we call poetry, and a poet with the precision that we call scientific.

Great scientists have always captured the imagination of poets. The alchemist of medieval times no less than the chemist, and the barber surgeon no less than the doctor have been the subjects of poems—not always flattering ones! Indeed, some of the epigrams satirizing stargazers, mathematicians, and especially doctors go back to Roman times, perhaps even earlier. The great majority of the poems, though, that have been written about scientists are hymns of praise. Some are so adulatory that we wonder whether any mortal could deserve such extravagant language. Sir Isaac Newton, in particular, has probably had more odes dedicated to him than have been inspired by all the nine Muses put together.

153

Shakespeare said:

> *"The lunatic, the lover and the poet*
> *Are of imagination all compact."*

This nimble verse has often been quoted to prove that poets are lunatics and that the paths of imagination lead but to the padded cell. But scientists themselves when describing their work almost always tell us that intuition plays a great part in their discoveries. Of course, intuition must be accompanied by months or even years of painstaking effort, some of which, tragically enough, comes to nothing.

The poems included here celebrate the human qualities of scientists, their courage, their compassion, and their integrity. If we were to try to find what manner of man a great scientist is we would in these poems see him as a suffering, striving human being, neither a god descended from Olympus nor a devil playing with fire—or uranium.

Some of the scientists who are the subjects of these poems are famous men, some, such as Mr. Attila and William Jones, have no local habitation except in the pages of a book. All of them, real and imaginary, are dedicated men, honest and humble.

THE SACRED ORDER

For George Sarton

Never forget this when the talk is clever:
Michelet suffered chaos in his bone
To bring to clarity the history of France.
His life-blood flowed into old documents.
The scholar at his desk burned like a lover.

At century's end behold the sceptic rules;
Doubt, like the tyrant's servants, seals
The visionary books. The scholar's passion,
His burning heart is wholly out of fashion.
The human spirit goes, the caste prevails.

Urbane and foxy, the professors shut
Up Michelet in his coffin and abandon
To entomologists the wild and living truth
To pin down in their books like any moth.
The mandarins come in, the men go out.

Now is detachment the supreme holy word
(Above all take no part nor risk your head);
Forgotten are Erasmus' pilgrimages
By these who fabricate and love their cages—
Has truth then never buckled on a sword?

Never forget this when the talk is clever:
Wisdom must be born in the flesh or wither,
And sacred order has been always won

From chaos by some burning faithful one
Whose human bones have ached as if with fever

To bring you to these high triumphant places.
Forget the formulas, remember men.
Praise scholars, for their never-ending story
Is written out in fire and this is their glory.
Read faith as on a lover's in their faces.

May Sarton

EPITAPH INTENDED FOR
SIR ISAAC NEWTON

Nature and Nature's laws lay hid in night:
God said, Let Newton be! and all was light.

Alexander Pope

NEWTON

From the Prelude, Book III

              . . . the statue stood
Of Newton with his prism and silent face,
The marble index of a mind for ever,
Voyaging through strange seas of Thought, alone.

William Wordsworth

from TO THE MEMORY OF
SIR ISAAC NEWTON

All-intellectual eye, our solar round
First gazing through; he by the blended power
Of gravitation and projection saw
The whole in silent harmony revolve.

    .   .   .   .

Th' aerial flow of Sound was known to him,
From whence it first in wavy circles breaks,
Till the touched organ takes the message in.
Nor could the darting beam, of speed immense,
Escape his swift pursuit and measuring eye.
Even Light itself, which every thing displays,
Shone undiscovered, till his brighter mind
Untwisted all the shining robe of day;
And, from the whitening undistinguished blaze,
Collecting every ray into his kind,
To the charmed eye educed the gorgeous train
Of parent colors.

James Thomson

"SIR HUMPHRY DAVY"

Sir Humphry Davy
Abominated gravy
He lived in the odium
Of having discovered sodium.

E. C. Bentley

THE FIFTIETH BIRTHDAY OF AGASSIZ

May 28, 1857

It was fifty years ago
　　In the pleasant month of May,
In the beautiful Pays de Vaud,
　　A child in its cradle lay.

And Nature, the old nurse, took
　　The child upon her knee,
Saying: "Here is a story-book
　　Thy Father has written for thee."

"Come, wander with me," she said,
　　"Into regions yet untrod;
And read what is still unread
　　In the manuscripts of God."

And he wandered away and away
　　With Nature, the dear old nurse,
Who sang to him night and day
　　The rhymes of the universe.

And whenever the way seemed long,
　　Or his heart began to fail,
She would sing a more wonderful song,
　　Or tell a more marvellous tale.

161

So she keeps him still a child,
    And will not let him go,
Though at times his heart beats wild
    For the beautiful Pays de Vaud;

Though at times he hears in his dreams
    The Ranz des Vaches of old,
And the rush of mountain streams
    From glaciers clear and cold;

And the mother at home says, "Hark!
    For his voice I listen and yearn;
It is growing late and dark,
    And my boy does not return!"

Henry Wadsworth Longfellow

A FAREWELL TO AGASSIZ

How the mountains talked together,
Looking down upon the weather,
When they heard our friend had planned his
Little trip among the Andes!
How they'll bare their snowy scalps
To the climber of the Alps
When the cry goes through their passes,
"Here comes the great Agassiz!"
"Yes, I'm tall," says Chimborazo,
"But I wait for him to say so,—
That's the only thing that lacks,—he
Must see me, Cotopaxi!"
"Ay! ay!" the fire-peak thunders,
"And he must view my wonders!
I'm but a lonely crater
Till I have him for spectator!"
The mountain hearts are yearning,
The lava-torches burning,
The rivers bend to meet him,
The forests bow to greet him,
It thrills the spinal column
Of fossil fishes solemn,
And glaciers crawl the faster
To the feet of their old master!
Heaven keep him well and hearty,
Both him and all his party!
From the sun that broils and smites,

From the centipede that bites,
From the hailstorm and the thunder,
From the vampire and the condor,
From the gust upon the river,
From the sudden earthquake shiver,
From the trip of mule or donkey,
From the midnight howling monkey,
From the stroke of knife or dagger,
From the puma and the jaguar,
From the horrid boa-constrictor
That has scared us in the pictur',
From the Indians of the Pampas
Who would dine upon their grampas,
From every beast and vermin
That to think of sets us squirmin',
From every snake that tries on
The traveller his p'ison,
From every pest of Natur',
Likewise the alligator,

   .   .   .   .   .

May he find, with his apostles,
That the land is full of fossils,
That the waters swarm with fishes
Shaped according to his wishes,
That every pool is fertile
In fancy kinds of turtle,
New birds around him singing,
New insects, never stinging,
With a million novel data

About the articulata,
And facts that strip off all husks
From the history of mollusks.

     . . . . .

Bless them head and heart and hand,
Till their glorious raid is o'er,
And they touch our ransomed shore!
Then the welcome of a nation,
With its shout of exultation,
Shall awake the dumb creation,
And the shapes of buried aeons
Join the living creatures' paeans,
Till the fossil echoes roar;
While the mighty megalosaurus
Leads the palaeozoic chorus,—
God bless the great Professor,
And the land his proud possessor,—
Bless them now and evermore!

Oliver Wendell Holmes

WILLIAM JONES

Once in a while a curious weed unknown to me,
Needing a name from my books;
Once in a while a letter from Yeomans.
Out of the mussel-shells gathered along the shore
Sometimes a pearl with a glint like meadow rue:
Then betimes a letter from Tyndall in England,
Stamped with the stamp of Spoon River.
I, lover of Nature, beloved for my love of her,
Held such converse afar with the great,
Who knew her better than I.
Oh, there is neither lesser nor greater,
Save as we make her greater and win from her keener delight.
With shells from the river cover me, cover me.
I lived in wonder, worshipping earth and heaven.
I have passed on the march eternal of endless life.

Edgar Lee Masters

LINES TO DR. DITMARS

*By one who observed him filling out his customs
declaration in the lounge of the S.S. Nerissa, September 6*

Here between lunch and teatime, and days and hours between
The wash from the Orinoco and the vast Sargasso green,
As I watch you sitting and brooding, fitfully biting your pen,
I wonder: Are you, too, tempted, even as other men?

Is it thoughts like these you are thinking, here on the ocean plain,
Far from the wave-washed Bocas, distant from Port of Spain,
When the last of the loveless Virgins has vanished into the sea:
"How many boa constrictors can I take in duty-free?

"Touching those fer-de-lances I found in that little place
—Why am I always chasing more than I meant to chase?—
Is it wrong to forget to declare them; would anyone count it amiss?
I could carry them in my pockets if only they wouldn't hiss!

"And my coral snakes, capital fellows"—your brow is creased in
    a frown—
"I fear I've exceeded my quota; do I *have* to put them down?
Why couldn't some of us *wear* them? Is anyone bound to know
That we didn't have them with us when we sailed three weeks ago?

"My vampire bats are no trouble"—your dark frown lightens and
    lifts—
"Touristy trifles, I'll grant you, but they *do* make excellent gifts.

And I hope that the chaps at Customs who rummage among my
    things
Will keep if they can from mussing my bushmaster's loops and
    rings."

The trade winds stir at the curtains; the dark is beginning to fall,
But your features are firm with a purpose: "No, I'll declare them
    all.
I never was good at deceiving, and what excuse could I make
If the man reached into my luggage and pulled out a nine-foot
    snake?

"Conscience is always conscience; if there's some slight duty to
    pay,
One doesn't come back from a journey with a bushmaster every
    day."
So you write out your declaration, with a firm, deliberate pen,
Down to the last little lizard, even as other men.

Kenneth Allan Robinson

A WELCOME TO
DR. BENJAMIN APTHORP GOULD

*On His Return from South America
After Fifteen Years Devoted to Cataloguing
the Stars of the Southern Hemisphere*

Read at the Dinner given at the Hotel Vendome, May 6, 1885

Once more Orion and the sister Seven
    Look on thee from the skies that hailed thy birth,—
How shall we welcome thee, whose home was heaven,
    From thy celestial wanderings back to earth?

Science has kept her midnight taper burning
    To greet thy coming with its vestal flame;
Friendship has murmured, "When art thou returning?"
    "Not yet! Not yet!" the answering message came.

Thine was unstinted zeal, unchilled devotion,
    While the blue realm had kingdoms to explore,—
Patience, like his who ploughed the unfurrowed ocean,
    Till o'er its margin loomed San Salvador.

Through the long nights I see thee ever waking,
    Thy footstool earth, thy roof the hemisphere,
While with thy griefs our weaker hearts are aching,
    Firm as thine equatorial's rock-based pier.

The souls that voyaged the azure depths before thee
    Watch with thy tireless vigils, all unseen,—
Tycho and Kepler bend benignant o'er thee,
    And with his toy-like tube the Florentine,—

He at whose word the orb that bore him shivered
  To find her central sovereignty disowned,
While the wan lips of priest and pontiff quivered,
  Their jargon stilled, their Baal disenthroned.

Flamsteed and Newton look with brows unclouded,
  Their strife forgotten with its faded scars,—
(Titans, who found the world of space too crowded
  To walk in peace among its myriad stars.)

All cluster round thee,—seers of earliest ages,
  Persians, Ionians, Mizraim's learned kings,
From the dim days of Shinar's hoary sages
  To his who weighed the planet's fluid rings.

And we, for whom the northern heavens are lighted,
  For whom the storm has passed, the sun has smiled,
Our clouds all scattered, all our stars united,
  We claim thee, clasp thee, like a long-lost child.

Fresh from the spangled vault's o'er-arching splendor,
  Thy lonely pillar, thy revolving dome,
In heartfelt accents, proud, rejoicing, tender,
  We bid thee welcome to thine earthly home!

Oliver Wendell Holmes

RICHARD TOLMAN'S UNIVERSE

Eddington's universe goes phut.
Richard Tolman's can open and shut.
Eddington's bursts without grace or tact,
But Tolman's swells and perhaps may contract.
All that Eddington can see
Is entropy, entropy, entropy.
But Tolman throws a punch to the jaw
Of the second thermodynamic law.
His heart, indeed, is comforted
When he sees a displacement toward the red,
And he at once sets up an equation
Which wholly alters the situation.
Give more rope! Give more rope!
Give more rope to the spectroscope.
Then catch Andromeda and hang her.
Tolman's a first-chop Doppleganger.
Tell me what Newton never knew,
Things about Messier 42.
In words of one syllable display
How Cepheid variables get that way.
Bring the criminal to the bar,
That stripped the atoms of Van Maanen's star.
Let me hear alpha particles clank.
Serve my electrons on a Planck.
And, no matter what sort of Hell has popped,
Let not the constant h be dropped.
For things grow nebulous to me,

Especially the nebulae.
Astrophysics is perfectly grand.
There's nothing in it I understand
Except that I'm stuck for better or worse
In Tolman's elastic universe.

Leonard Bacon

THE STAR-SPLITTER

'You know Orion always comes up sideways.
Throwing a leg up over our fence of mountains,
And rising on his hands, he looks in on me
Busy outdoors by lantern-light with something
I should have done by daylight, and indeed,
After the ground is frozen, I should have done
Before it froze, and a gust flings a handful
Of waste leaves at my smoky lantern chimney
To make fun of my way of doing things,
Or else fun of Orion's having caught me.
Has a man, I should like to ask, no rights
These forces are obliged to pay respect to?'
So Brad McLaughlin mingled reckless talk
Of heavenly stars with hugger-mugger farming,
Till having failed at hugger-mugger farming,
He burned his house down for the fire insurance
And spent the proceeds on a telescope
To satisfy a life-long curiosity
About our place among the infinities.

'What do you want with one of those blame things?'
I asked him well beforehand. 'Don't you get one!'
'Don't call it blamed; there isn't anything
More blameless in the sense of being less
A weapon in our human fight,' he said.
'I'll have one if I sell my farm to buy it.'
There where he moved the rocks to plow the ground

And plowed between the rocks he couldn't move,
Few farms changed hands; so rather than spend years
Trying to sell his farm and then not selling,
He burned his house down for the fire insurance
And bought the telescope with what it came to.
He had been heard to say by several:
'The best thing that we're put here for's to see;
The strongest thing that's given us to see with's
A telescope. Someone in every town
Seems to me owes it to the town to keep one.
In Littleton it may as well be me.'
After such loose talk it was no surprise
When he did what he did and burned his house down.

Mean laughter went about the town that day
To let him know we weren't the least imposed on,
And he could wait—we'd see to him to-morrow.
But the first thing next morning we reflected
If one by one we counted people out
For the least sin, it wouldn't take us long
To get so we had no one left to live with.
For to be social is to be forgiving.
Our thief, the one who does our stealing from us,
We don't cut off from coming to church suppers,
But what we miss we go to him and ask for.
He promptly gives it back, that is if still
Uneaten, unworn out, or undisposed of.
It wouldn't do to be too hard on Brad
About his telescope. Beyond the age
Of being given one's gift for Christmas,

He had to take the best way he knew how
To find himself in one. Well, all we said was
He took a strange thing to be roguish over.
Some sympathy was wasted on the house,
A good old-timer dating back along;
But a house isn't sentient; the house
Didn't feel anything. And if it did,
Why not regard it as a sacrifice,
And an old-fashioned sacrifice by fire,
Instead of a new-fashioned one at auction?

Out of a house and so out of a farm
At one stroke (of a match), Brad had to turn
To earn a living on the Concord railroad,
As under-ticket-agent at a station
Where his job, when he wasn't selling tickets,
Was setting out up track and down, not plants
As on a farm, but planets, evening stars
That varied in their hue from red to green.

He got a good glass for six hundred dollars.
His new job gave him leisure for star-gazing.
Often he bid me come and have a look
Up the brass barrel, velvet black inside,
At a star quaking in the other end.
I recollect a night of broken clouds
And underfoot snow melted down to ice,
And melting further in the wind to mud.
Bradford and I had out the telescope.
We spread our two legs as we spread its three,

175

Pointed our thoughts the way we pointed it,
And standing at our leisure till the day broke,
Said some of the best things we ever said.
That telescope was christened the Star-splitter,
Because it didn't do a thing but split
A star in two or three the way you split
A globule of quicksilver in your hand
With one stroke of your finger in the middle.
It's a star-splitter if there ever was one
And ought to do some good if splitting stars
'Sa thing to be compared with splitting wood.
We've looked and looked, but after all where are we?
Do we know any better where we are,
And how it stands between the night to-night
And a man with a smoky lantern chimney?
How different from the way it ever stood?

Robert Frost

MR. ATTILA

They made a myth of you, professor,
   you of the gentle voice,
   the books, the specs,
   the furtive rabbit manners
   in the mortar-board cap
   and the medieval gown.

They didn't think it, eh professor?
On account of you're so absent-minded,
you bumping into the tree and saying,
"Excuse me, I thought you were a tree,"
passing on again blank and absent-minded.

Now it's "Mr. Attila, how do you do?"
Do you pack wallops of wholesale death?
Are you the practical dynamic son-of-a-gun?
Have you come through with a few abstractions?
Is it you Mr. Attila we hear saying,
"I beg your pardon but we believe we have made some degree
   of progress on the residual qualities of the atom"?

                            Carl Sandburg
                          (August, 1945)

from GIBBS

It was much later in his life he rose
in the professors' room, the frail bones rising
among that fume of mathematical meaning,
symbols, the language of symbols, literature . . . threw
air, simple life, in the dead lungs of their meeting,
said, "Mathematics *is* a language."

. . . . .

. . . . The yellow window
of Sloane Lab all night shone.

Shining an image whole, as a streak of brightness
bland on the quartz, light-blade on Iceland spar
doubled! and the refraction carrying fresh clews.

Muriel Rukeyser

HOMAGE TO THE PHILOSOPHER

For A. N. Whitehead

Some things persist by suffering change, others
Endure: the mountain endures, endures and is worn down, after
    ages is gone.
But nature, the philosopher tells his brothers,
Offers another fact for them to brood upon:
Eternal objects.   Color is such a one.

"It haunts time like a spirit. It comes and goes.
But when it comes," he reminds them, "it is the same
Color."
        These are years when even a child knows
Endurance.   And the famished face of a war with no name
Persists through change.   Yet there is a godlike game

For us to play, here, now.   The eternal objects are
Our counters.   Let our board be the ground,
Planted or paved, or the sea or the sky.   In particular
And passing forms—color, shape, sound
Surround us, physical, fantasied, lost, and found.

Eternal red, orange eternal too, yellow, green, blue,
Eternal violet.   Play with them, share their estate, set
Them up in the mind like circles and squares, like notes remaining
    true
Whether absent or there.   They will vanish, not die,
    even if you forget
Red, orange, yellow, green, eternal blue, eternal violet.

Babette Deutsch

179

EINSTEIN (1929)

He lies upon his bed
Exerting on Arcturus and the moon
Forces proportional inversely to
The squares of their remoteness and conceives
The universe.
      Atomic.
          He can count
Ocean in atoms and weigh out the air
In multiples of one and subdivide
Light to its numbers.
          If they will not speak
Let them be silent in their particles.
Let them be dead and he will lie among
Their dust and cipher them—undo the signs
Of their unreal identities and free
The pure and single factor of all sums—
Solve them to unity.

Archibald MacLeish

THE GIFT TO BE SIMPLE

Breathing something German at the end,
Which no one understood, he died, a friend,
   Or so he meant to be, to all of us.
   Only the stars defined his radius;
His life, restricted to a wooden house,
Was in his head. He saw a fledgling fall.
   Two times he tried to nest it, but it fell
   Once more, and died; he wandered home again—
We save so plain a story for great men.
      An angel in ill-fitting sweaters,
      Writing children naïve letters,
   A violin player lacking vanities,
   A giant wit among the homilies—
We have no parallel to that immense
        Intelligence.

But if he were remembered for the Bomb,
As some may well remember him, such a tomb,
   For one who hated violence and ceremony
   Equally, would be a wasted irony.
He flew to formal heavens from his perch,
A scientist become his own research,
   And even if the flames were never gold
   That lapped his body to an ash gone cold,
   Even if his death no trumpets tolled,
      There is enough of myth inside the truth
      To make a monument to fit him with;

And since the universe is in a jar,
There is no weeping where his heavens are,
And I would remember, now the world is less,
His gentleness.

Howard Moss

IN THE EVENING

In Memoriam Frederici Treves, 1853–1923

In the evening, when the world knew he was dead,
   He lay amid the dust and hoar
Of ages; and to a spirit attending said:
     "This chalky bed?—
I surely seem to have been here before?"

"O yes. You have been here. You knew the place,
   Substanced as you, long ere your call:
And if you cared to do so you might trace
     In this gray space
Your being, and the being of men all."

Thereto said he: "Then why was I called away?
   I knew no trouble or discontent:
Why did I not prolong my ancient stay
     Herein for aye?"
The spirit shook its head.—"None knows: you went,

"And though, perhaps, Time did not sign to you
   The need to go, dream-vision sees
How Aesculapius' phantom hither flew,
     With Galen's, too,
And his of Cos-plague-proof Hippocrates,

"And beckoned you forth, whose skill had read as theirs
　　Maybe, had Science chanced to spell
In their day, modern modes to stem despairs
　　That mankind bears!
Enough.　　You have returned.　　And all is well."

Dorchester Cemetery, January 2, 1924

Thomas Hardy

THE MASTER

(*September 29th, 1954*)

Master, whose fire kindled our glad surprise,
brought tropic seas to drear dissecting room,
so that we heard the thunder and the boom
of surf on reef—and hark, the boobies' cries—
or vitalised some skull, unwound its scroll,
or brought some fossil form to life again,
or thread of nerve in pickled flesh to pain,
you made the living and the dead one whole.
So when we wandered all the earth we sensed
your voice and watched your clear-cut features play,
pausing, perhaps, in moments of that bliss
of finding some rare thing, triumphant, tensed,
seeking to share our joy, then would we say,
"What would I give to hear Wood Jones on this!"

C.G.L.

HEART SPECIALIST

For M.P.

His house is a haven where fingers dare
Push at a doorbell that sounds like a prayer
For in his brain, his subtle hand,
Are gifts that help him understand
The grip of pride on a flimsy cane,
Halting step, futile guile,
Mumbled word, dubious smile,
The unbelievable path of pain.

In diagrams a pulse conveys
The manuscript of numbered days;
Triumphal march and epitaph
Are only tracings on a graph.

He knows that a span of time may vary
As a pin point of space in a coronary,
That even death can be no stronger
Than the will of a muscle to beat on longer,
And so he serves as philosopher friend
When the winds blow chill at the season's end,
When life comes fumbling at his door,
A wastrel who can spend no more.

Elias Lieberman

186

LINES WRITTEN AFTER THE DISCOVERY
BY THE AUTHOR
OF THE GERM OF YELLOW FEVER

This day relenting God
    Hath placed within my hand
A wondrous thing; and God
    Be praised. At His command,

Seeking His secret deeds
    With tears and toiling breath,
I find thy cunning seeds,
    O million-murdering Death.

I know this little thing
    A myriad men will save.
O Death, where is thy sting?
    Thy victory, O Grave?

Ronald Ross

A CORRECT COMPASSION

To Mr. Philip Allison, after watching him perform a Mitral
Stenosis Valvulotomy in the General Infirmary at Leeds.

Cleanly, sir, you went to the core of the matter.
Using the purest kind of wit, a balance of belief and art,
You with a curious nervous elegance laid bare
The root of life, and put your finger on its beating heart.

The glistening theatre swarms with eyes, and hands, and eyes.
On green-clothed tables, ranks of instruments transmit a sterile
    gleam.
The masks are on, and no unnecessary smile betrays
A certain tension, true concomitant of calm.

Here we communicate by looks, though words,
Too, are used, as in continuous historic present
You describe our observations and your deeds.
All gesture is reduced to its result, an instrument.

She who does not know she is a patient lies
Within a tent of green, and sleeps without a sound
Beneath the lamps, and the reflectors that devise
Illuminations probing the profoundest wound.

A calligraphic master, improvising, you invent
The first incision, and no poet's hesitation
Before his snow-blank page mars your intent:
The flowing stroke is drawn like an uncalculated inspiration.

A garland of flowers unfurls across the painted flesh.
With quick precision the arterial forceps click.
Yellow threads are knotted with a simple flourish.
Transfused, the blood preserves its rose, though it is sick.

Meters record the blood, measure heart-beats, control the breath.
Hieratic gesture: scalpel bares a creamy rib; with pincer knives
The bone quietly is clipped, and lifted out. Beneath,
The pink, black-mottled lung like a revolted creature heaves,

Collapses; as if by extra fingers is neatly held aside
By two ordinary egg-beaters, kitchen tools that curve
Like extraordinary hands. Heart, laid bare, silently beats. It can
    hide
No longer yet is not revealed.—'A local anaesthetic in the cardiac
    nerve.'

Now, in firm hands that quiver with a careful strength,
Your knife feels through the heart's transparent skin; at first,
Inside the pericardium, slit down half its length,
The heart, black-veined, swells like a fruit about to burst,

But goes on beating, love's poignant image bleeding at the dart
Of a more grievous passion, as a bird, dreaming of flight, sleeps on
Within its leafy cage.—'It generally upsets the heart
A bit, though not unduly, when I make the first injection.'

Still, still the patient sleeps, and still the speaking heart is dumb.
The watchers breathe an air far sweeter, rarer than the room's.
The cold walls listen. Each in his own blood hears the drum
She hears, tented in green, unfathomable calms.

'I make a purse-string suture here, with a reserve
Suture, which I must make first, and deeper,
As a safeguard, should the other burst. In the cardiac nerve
I inject again a local anaesthetic. Could we have fresh towels to
    cover

All these adventitious ones? Now can you all see?
When I put my finger inside the valve, there may be a lot
Of blood, and it may come with quite a bang. But I let it flow,
In case there are any clots, to give the heart a good clean-out.

Now can you give me every bit of light you've got?'
We stand on the benches, peering over his shoulder.
The lamp's intensest rays are concentrated on an inmost heart.
Someone coughs. 'If you have to cough, you will do it outside this
    theatre.'—'Yes, sir.'

'How's she breathing, Doug? Do you feel quite happy?'— 'Yes,
    fairly
Happy.'—'Now. I am putting my finger in the opening of the
    valve.
I can only get the tip of my finger in.—It's gradually
Giving way.—I'm inside.—No clots.—I can feel the valve

Breathing freely now around my finger, and the heart working.
Not too much blood. It opened very nicely.
I should say that anatomically speaking
This is a perfect case.—Anatomically.

190

For of course, anatomy is not physiology.'
We find we breathe again, and hear the surgeon hum.
Outside, in the street, a car starts up. The heart regularly
Thunders.—'I do not stitch up the pericardium.

It is not necessary.'—For this is imagination's other place,
Where only necessary things are done, with the supreme and grave
Dexterity that ignores technique; with proper grace
Informing a correct compassion, that performs its love, and makes
  it live.

James Kirkup

INDEX OF AUTHORS

Auden, W. H., 91

Bacon, Leonard, 171
Benét, Stephen Vincent, 115
Bentley, E. C., 160
Bishop, John Peale, 25
Bishop, Morris, 82, 132
Blake, William, 5
Blunden, Edmund, 71
Bogan, Louise, 111
Bragdon, Claude, 89
Branch, Anna Hempstead, 72
Butler, Samuel, 23, 86

C. G. L., 185
Ciardi, John, 24
Coatsworth, Elizabeth, 31
Coffin, Robert P. Tristram, 83, 108
Colum, Padraic, 76
Crane, Stephen, 139

Day, Clarence, 125
de la Mare, Walter, 137
Denney, Reuel, 70
Deutsch, Babette, 149, 179
Dickinson, Emily, 21, 107, 141, 144
Dillon, George, 127

Eliot, T. S., 6
Emerson, Ralph Waldo, 8, 34

Frost, Robert, 104, 113, 173

Gardner, Isabella, 105
Guiterman, Arthur, 29

Hardy, Thomas, 140, 183
Herrick, Robert, 61
Holmes, Oliver Wendell, 163, 169
Housman, A. E., 37, 77

Jeffers, Robinson, 53

Kirkup, James, 32, 188

Lamb, Charles, 110
Lieberman, Elias, 186
Lindsay, Vachel, 81
Longfellow, Henry Wadsworth, 161
Lucretius, 9

MacLeish, Archibald, 55, 62, 180
McCord, David, 27, 51, 130
Martial, 119
Masefield, John, 136
Masters, Edgar Lee, 166
Melville, Herman, 128
Millay, Edna St. Vincent, 75, 133
Moore, Marianne, 67, 84, 147
Moss, Howard, 181

Nash, Ogden, 120
Nicholl, Louise Townsend, 26, 36, 52, 142
Nicholson, Norman, 38

Pope, Alexander, 121, 157

Raine, Kathleen, 42, 43, 44, 99
Rich, Adrienne Cecile, 30
Robinson, Kenneth Allan, 167
Ross, Ronald, 187

Rounds, Emma, 87
Rukeyser, Muriel, 178

Sandburg, Carl, 78, 177
Sarton, May, 155
Shakespeare, William, 22
Shelley, Percy Bysshe, 12, 46
Spencer, Theodore, 90
Speyer, Leonora, 146
Sully-Prudhomme, 63, 69

Taylor, Bert Leston, 112
Tennyson, Alfred, Lord, 33, 126, 131

Thomas, Dylan, 98
Thompson, Francis, 50
Thomson, James, 159
Thoreau, Henry, 49, 124
Traherne, Thomas, 145

Van Doren, Mark, 19, 102
Vaughn, Henry, 7

Welles, Winifred, 17
White, E. B., 65
Wordsworth, William, 85, 158
Wylie, Elinor, 18, 103

INDEX OF TITLES

Apostrophic Notes from the New-World Physics, 65
Arithmetic, 78
Ark of the Covenant, 36
"Atom from Atom," 8
At Woodward's Gardens, 113
Auguries of Innocence, 5

Cloud, the, 46
Cold-Blooded Creatures, 103
Continent's End, 53
Correct Compassion, a, 188

Different Speech, a, 26
Dinosaur, the, 112
Dunce, the, 137

$E = MC^2$, 82
Einstein (1929), 180
Entropy, 90
Epilogue, 128
Epistle to Be Left in the Earth, 55
Epitaph Intended for Sir Isaac Newton, 157
Essay on Man, an, 121
Euclid, 81
"Euclid Alone Has Looked on Beauty Bare," 75

Farewell to Agassiz, a, 163
Fiftieth Birthday of Agassiz, the, 161

For the Conjunction of Two Planets, 30
Force That Through the Green Fuse Drives the Flower, the, 98
Four Quartets, 6
Four Quartz Crystal Clocks, 67
Funebrial Reflections, 120

Genesis, Chapter 1, 14
Gibbs, 178
Gift to Be Simple, the, 181
God of Galaxies, the, 19
"God's First Creature Was Light," 17
Go Fly a Saucer, 27

Heart Specialist, 186
Heredity, 140
Homage to the Philosopher, 179
Hudibras, Canto I, 86
Hudibras, Canto III, 23

Icosasphere, the, 84
If They Spoke, 102
In Memoriam, CXX, 131
In Memoriam, CXXXI, 126
Innate Helium, 104
In the Evening, 183
"I Saw a Peacock," 106
It Rolls On, 132

Job, Chapter 36, 45
Job, Chapter 38, 39
Journal, 133

Laboratory Midnight, the, 70
Lines to Dr. Ditmars, 167
Lines Written After the Discovery by the Author of the Germ of Yellow Fever, 187
"Low-Anchored Cloud," 49

"Man Is But a Castaway," 125
Man Said to the Universe, a, 139
Masked Shrew, the, 105
Master, the, 185
Mathematics or the Gift of Tongues, 72
"Men Say They Know Many Things," 124
Message from Home, 99
Metropolitan Nightmare, 115
Mr. Attila, 177
Motion of the Earth, the, 38
My Father's Watch, 24

Naked World, the, 69
Newton, 158
New York—December, 1931, 149
Non Amo Te, 119
"No Single Thing Abides," 9
Numbers and Faces, 91

Ode to the Hayden Planetarium, 29
Once a Child, 21
Our Little Kinsmen, 107

Physical Geography, 52
Plane Geometry, 87
Pleiades, the, 31
"Point, the," 89
Prelude, the; Book VI, 85
Princess, the, 33
Progress, 130
Prometheus Unbound, 12
Psalm 8, 150

Relativity, 64
Reliques, 71
"Remember, Though the Telescope Extend," 127
Reply to Mr. Wordsworth, 62
Revolution, 37
Richard Tolman's Universe, 171
Rock, 42

Sacred Order, the, 155
"Science in God," 61
Shape of the Heart, the, 142
Shells, 43
Sir Humphry Davy, 160
Spider, the, 108
Staff of Aesculapius, the, 147
Starfish, the, 83
Star-Splitter, the, 173
"Surgeons Must Be Very Careful," 144

Thanksgiving for the Body, 145
"There Was a Young Man from Trinity," 80
"There Was an Old Man Who Said, 'Do'," 79
This Dim and Ptolemaic Man, 25
To a Snow-Flake, 50
Tortoise in Eternity, the, 18
To the Memory of Sir Isaac Newton, 159
"To Think That Two and Two Are Four," 77
Triumph of the Whale, the, 110
Troilus and Cressida, 22
Tulips, 76

Ursa Major, 32

Vision, a, 7
Variation on a Sentence, 111

196

Water, 44
Wealth, 34
Weather Words, 51
Welcome to Dr. Benjamin Apthorp
    Gould, a, 169
"What Am I, Life," 136

Wheel, the, 63
William Jones, 166
(With a Daisy), 141

X-Ray, 146

INDEX OF FIRST LINES

Age being mathematical, these flowers, an, 76

All-intellectual eye, our solar round, 159

Among the anthropophagi, 120

And mathematics, fresh as May, 71

And 'Science' said, 137

And, star and system rolling past, 126

Animals will never know, the, 102

Arithmetic is where numbers fly like pigeons in and out of your head, 78

Atom from atom yawns as far, 8

At the equinox when the earth was veiled in a late rain, 53

Behold, God is great, and we know him not, 45

Behold the mighty dinosaur, 112

Boy, presuming on his intellect, a, 113

Breathing something German at the end, 181

By special lens, photo-electric cells, 26

Child's cough scratches at my heart —my head, the, 149

Cleanly, sir, you went to the core of the matter, 188

Darwin and Mendel laid on man the chains, 130

Day with sky so wide, a, 38

Do you remember, when you were first a child, 99

Eddington's universe goes phut, 171

Egyptians say, The Sun has twice, the, 23

Euclid alone has looked on Beauty bare, 75

Far as creation's ample range extends, 121

Force that through the green fuse drives the flower, the, 98

For forty years, for forty-one, 25

From dark the striped muscles sprang, 17

God of galaxies has more to govern, the, 19

Heavens themselves, the planets and this centre, the, 22

He lies upon his bed, 180

Here between lunch and teatime, and days and hours between, 167

His house is a haven where fingers dare, 186

How the mountains talked together, 163

I am the family face, 140

I bring fresh showers for the thirsting flowers, 46

I do not love thee, Dr. Fell, 119
If Luther's day expand to Darwin's year, 128
I know four winds with names like some strange tune, 51
I looked into my body, 146
'In Buckinghamshire hedgerows,' 84
In Mathematicks he was greater, 86
In the beginning God created the heaven and the earth, 14
In the evening, when the world knew he was dead, 183
Io! Paean! Io! sing, 110
I read with varying degrees, 133
I saw a peacock with a fiery tail, 106
I saw Eternity the other night, 7
It is colder now, 55
It rained quite a lot that spring, 115
I trust I have not wasted breath, 131
It troubled me as once I was, 21
It was fifty years ago, 161
It was much later in his life he rose, 178
I've seen one flying saucer. Only when, 27

Kingdom of Number is all boundaries, the, 91

Light has come again and found, 36
Low-anchored cloud, 49

Man, the egregious egoist, 103
Man is but a castaway, 125
Man said to the universe, a, 139
Master, whose fire kindled our glad surprise, 185
Matter whose movement moves us all, 90
Men say they know many things, 124

Nature and Nature's laws lay hid in night, 157
Never forget this when the talk is clever, 155
No single thing abides; but all things flow, 9

O Lord, 145
Of white and tawny, black as ink, 111
Old Euclid drew a circle, 81
Once in a while a curious weed unknown to me, 166
Once more Orion and the sister Seven, 169
One night I dreamed I was locked in my Father's watch, 24
Our little kinsmen after rain, 107

Penny is heavier than the shrew, a, 105
Point, the line, the surface and the sphere, the, 89

Reaching down arm-deep into bright water, 43
Religious faith is a most filling vapor, 104
Remember, though the telescope extend, 127

Science—so the savants say, a, 141
Science in God, is known to be, 61
Science is what the world is, earth and water, 70
Shape of the heart is an old design, the, 142
Sir Humphry Davy, 160
Slung between the homely poplars at the end, 32
Some things persist by suffering change, others, 179

199

Space-time, our scientists tell us, is impervious, 62

Sphere, which is as many thousand spheres, a, 12

Statue stood, the, 158

Sudden refreshment came upon the school, 52

Surgeons must be very careful, 144

Surrounded by beakers, by strange coils, 69

Sweet as violets to a weary heart, 31

Sweet reader, whom I've never seen, 65

Symbol from the first, of mastery, a, 147

There are four vibrators, the world's exactest clocks, 67

There is a stream that flowed before the first beginning, 44

There is stone in me that knows stone, 42

There was an old man who said, "Do," 79

There was a young lady named Bright, 64

There was a young man from Trinity, 80

They made a myth of you, professor, 177

This day relenting God, 187

This is the time of wonder, it is written, 132

This is the Word whose breaking heart, 72

This world was once a fluid haze of light, 33

'Tis told by one whom stormy waters threw, 85

To see a World in a grain of sand, 5

To think that two and two are four, 77

Triangles are commands of God, 83

'Twas Euclid, and the theorem pi, 87

We shall not cease from exploration, 6

We smile at astrological hopes, 30

West and away the wheels of darkness roll, 37

What am I, Life? A thing of watery salt, 136

What heart could have thought you, 50

What was our trust, we trust not, 82

Wheel's inventor, nameless demi-god, the, 63

When I consider thy heavens, the work of thy fingers, 150

Where wast thou when I laid the foundations of the earth, 39

Who shall tell what did befall, 34

Within my house of patterned horn, 18

With six small diamonds for his eyes, 108

'You know Orion always comes up sideways,' 173